SOLE SEARCHING

Recollections of an Unexceptional Hiker

Jeff Herald

Books by Jeff Herald:

Sole Searching

Recollections of an Unexceptional Hiker

For Love and Freedom

<u>The Cody Dillon Saga</u>

PERIPHERAL VISIONS

Cody Dillon-The Saga Begins

BANNACK

Cody Dillon-The Saga Continues

CALABASH

Cody Dillon-The Third Law

THE MESA BEYOND

Cody Dillon - In My Image

This book is meant to be a slightly humorous memoir of a few experiences in my life. Some names, characteristics and places may have been changed and events compressed. I make no guarantee that I have told the truth - the whole truth - and nothing but the truth. However, in the best sense, these stories are recalled to the best of my recollection and penned with the expressed intent of boosting the egos of, and entertaining all named participants. While some of the participants named within may have differing recollections of these events, I'm pretty sure mine are considerably more factual.

I welcome any comments and questions. Feel free to contact me and discuss hiking, trails and camping at the email below.

Jeff Herald
flailingturtle@yahoo.com

ACKNOWLEDGMENTS

No book writes itself. And I would suppose that very few books are written and reach the publishing phase without the input and help from others beyond the author. This is certainly true for these pages. First and foremost I would like to thank my wife, DeAnne and my daughter, Sarah for their constant encouragement, valuable insights, and for enduring my personal tunnel vision from this book's inception.

There are a few wonderful people who have willingly given their time to read and in many cases, offer editing advice along with kind encouragement freely. The advice has been gratefully accepted and I have gained much due to your kind and helpful assistance. A special thanks to each of you.

Tony Caffarelli
Alexis Eliot
Rilla (Mom) Herald
Larry Herald
DeAnne Herald
Sarah Herald
Linda Luvaas
Donna Tricou

Photos courtesy of:
Larry Herald
Justin Herald
Sarah Herald
Jeff Herald

Last but certainly not least, there are a select group of people that have made these and many other untold stories a part of my truly wonderful life on many trails and in countless camps. You have all shared and enriched my days communing with nature, as well as endured my trail-bound whining, poor directional guidance and lack of physical preparedness. It is with great pleasure and much thankfulness that I count you as hiking and camping compadres.

Richard (Dad) Herald
Bob Herald
Larry Herald
DeAnne Herald
Sarah Herald
Justin Herald
Jaclyn Herald
Matt Herald
Kristen Herald
Bob Weyandt

In memory of Bob Herald

Wherever we go in the mountains we find more than we seek. - John Muir

Forward

"One day I undertook a tour through the country, and the diversity and beauties of nature I met with in this charming season, expelled every gloomy and vexatious thought." ~ Daniel Boone

The journey through life has a tendency to wear many of us down. It doesn't really matter much what we do, after a while we question the validity of our existence, or at least of our daily routines. Pulling the same levers, pushing the same buttons, typing letter after letter, unloading truck after truck, verifying forms, investigating crime, planting the same fields, any of it can become an echo reverberating over and over again until we just want to silence the drone.

I tend to be a positive guy. One reason being that my life has been blessed, dilemmas being few and far between. It could also be partly because I tend to look past troubles and tribulations. I focus on that sliver of sun shining brightly, warming my face and brightening the colors of my immediate surroundings, not the cloud that is obscuring the other ninety percent and casting shadows over the rest of the visible world. I'll give you an example.

Before we were married, Dee and I worked, ate lunch and spent our free time together seven days a week from almost the minute she was hired and moved to my rural hometown of Wooster, Ohio. We married, went on our honeymoon and upon our return to work a week later, we were both told we would be transferred to different divisions within our twenty company corporation, both at corporate headquarters in downtown Cleveland, Ohio. Now I had worked for sixteen years in the same building, known within the corporation as the "country club" due to its green grass, beautiful trees and small town setting.

Prior to being transferred, I would occasionally have to drive to a meeting at our corporate HQ, fifty miles north, on East 55th Street in Cleveland. On the way to one particular meeting, I rode with a fellow employee. As we weaved through stop and go traffic in view of the city skyline, I remember telling him that if I ever had to drive into the city every day, I would be depressed enough to end it all. I'm telling you I hate cities. Oh sure, many have tremendous history, impressive buildings and a myriad of interesting activities and entertainment. These are not a draw to me.

The point I wish to make here is that Dee and I both strived to embrace the city's positives, many of which I just mentioned along with the fact that; Number one - we both still had jobs... Number two - we were able to ride to work, eat lunch and return home, together. That was the sliver of sunshine peeking out from behind that large looming cloud known as the City of Cleveland and the one hundred mile round trip daily commute. Don't get me wrong, as cities go, Cleveland is a pretty good one. As far as places I wanted to spend ten or so hours of my life every day, I can assure you, NO city is on my wish list. But we survived and enjoyed it as much as we could.

X

The real saving grace for us was the fact that every day we returned to the secluded woodsy refuge we called home. Thanks to friends of my parents, we were lucky enough to rent a house deep in a wooded valley, complete with a several acre yard, a half-acre spring fed pond, a high stony cliff, steep surrounding hillsides and around seventy five wooded acres bordered by a swift flowing stream. Talk about light at the end of the daily tunnel...home was an open-armed, natural sanctuary beckoning us on our southerly drive down I71 toward quiet, private, sanity. That place rejuvenated our souls and filled us with a sense of adventure and wonder. Being there quieted the drone. We are grateful for the time we were able to spend there.

Nature, the woods, mountains, and rivers, I always enjoyed my times in such places. However, it took me a few years to understand that their aura... *expelled every gloomy and vexatious thought."*

XIII

SOLE SEARCHING

Recollections of an Unexceptional Hiker

XIV

Contents

Chapter 1
Boys Will be Boys

rugs, miniskirts, rock music, Vietnam, the cold war, demonstrations, space exploration, and advancing technology defined the times. The 1960's and 70's...It was different then. But, I was too busy to be bogged down by such serious subjects. Well, being somewhat honest about it, miniskirts and music probably did catch some of my attention. Ok, ok...a lot of my attention!

I mentioned the cold war. The Soviet Block and the good old US of A were in a dangerous nuclear arms race. News reports and adult conversations bombarded us with the dangers of political espionage, military threats, bluffs, or worse yet, military action. Ever-present fears of either side lobbing a nuclear-armed ballistic missile, thus setting off WWIII and the end of the world, blanketed the country like a foreboding black cloud. Some families even built personal bomb shelters in their back yards. Towns and cities had designated fallout shelters. Schools performed bomb drills and I remember being made to crouch under my desk for protection, referred to as duck and cover. Have you ever seen those early newsreels of a plywood, model town disintegrating in a 10 million-degree, 1000 mile per hour nuclear-wind during a test blast? We were shown those, and I wasn't really buying that hiding under a maple desk top, with names carved in it from 1943, would save me during a nuke strike. There, now you know I tended to be skeptical at times. Apprehension and fear ruled. Look up the 1962 Cuban missile crisis and you will get the idea. It was scary and it all sucked. I made the unconscious choice to continue with life despite those negative worldly influences.

I was born in 1956 and therefore young and naive during those decades. My brother, Larry, was just 18 months younger. We were pretty much constant companions. Most days were filled with mindless roaming, sports, games, and in general, growing up in small town America.

Wooster, Ohio, population around 15,000, was a rural, small college town in Wayne County. The College of Wooster, founded as Wooster University in 1866, began operating in 1870. It is still there today with an enrollment of around 2000. The county was largely agricultural. As I recall, dairy, corn, and potatoes, were the primary commodities.. Yep...that was home.

Larry and I often camped in the wilds of our North Eastern Ohio back yard. Ok, there were houses on all sides of our 1/2-acre yard, and paved county roads just a couple houses away to our north and south. We were brothers, and sometimes a friend or two, roughing it in the great outdoors. We survived with the aid of hot dogs, chips, flashlights, transistor AM radio, army surplus canteens of water, and sleeping bags. Home for the night was an army surplus, olive drab, canvass wall tent complete with wooden poles, steel pegs and no floor. That tent was a great outdoor abode, weighing in at around 350 pounds! Well, it felt like 350 pounds.

We laid out, watching the sky for shooting stars and possible UFOs...it was the 1960s you know! It was only 20 years after the Roswell, New Mexico flying saucer crash. The validity of both the original official US Army Air Force press release of the "saucer crash", or the next day's official retraction/explanation are still being hotly debated to this day. Weather balloon my ass! Perhaps I'll share more on such ideas later. Anyway, we always had eyes to the sky!

Black and white TV allowed us to watch our favorite shows like "The Man from Uncle". The neighbors were surely intrigued as they watched me slink stealthily through our back yard, from tree stump to concealing bushes, sporting my plastic, triangular "U.N.C.L.E." ID badge while wielding my plastic semi-automatic pistol, complete with removable silencer and buttstock. Yep, we engaged in a little espionage of our own!

Advancements in technology gave us the hand sized transistor radio, complete with a single ear-bud, opening up the musical and sports wonders of the world. On a good clear night we could pick up radio stations from as far off as New Orleans, St. Louis, Dallas and Nashville. Heck, it was like traveling around the country on airwaves. Famous

DJ, Wolfman Jack, played the latest rock and roll...how cool was that!

Camping adventures included sneaking off in the middle of the night and walking to the local gravel pit where we would skip stones, discuss important life events (girls, sports and such), and sneak a cigarette or two...again, it was the 60s you know! Heck, just watch a movie or television show produced in those days, everybody lit up a Marlboro every 30 seconds or so. It seemed like the thing to do. We wanted to be cool too.

On occasion we would quietly head off on our bikes for a nocturnal excursion on the back roads. Exploring the countryside in the dark, on a bike, was high adventure. We were alert, avoiding all traffic, especially Sheriff patrol cars (well usually). It all gave us a feeling of living on the edge. There was that one time...a 10- mile night ride was near completion, when I and two friends, (who shall remain nameless to protect their innocence), crested the last rise on route 3 when one of us noticed a car's parking lights, 1/4- mile on down the road. We stopped right there in the road, under a streetlight...dumb. As you might have guessed, headlights and flashing reds (blue lights were not a thing at that time) glared, as that car raced towards us. Yep...we threw our bikes in the ditch and took off running through back yards, like bats out of hell. We knew that neighborhood like the back of our hands. We zigged as the patrol car zagged. We could see the flashing lights in some of our neighbors' driveways, always two steps behind us. No way they could catch us. Back at the tent, we laughed between gasps for air. Bullet dodged! Then it hit me, he had our bikes. How would I explain that to Mom and Dad?... *"Hey Mom, Dad, my bike went missing last night...maybe the Sheriff's Department was collecting them for needy kids."* We decided, after some heated debate, surrender was the best course of action. Unbelievably, when we got there it was all clear. Sweet, our bikes were still in the ditch! I reached for my bike, and at the last second, a large, black uniformed, shiny badged, flashlight wielding, Deputy Sheriff jumped from the weeds! He nabbed me... initiating my life of crime. I could see Barney Fife, slamming the cell door..."no more carefree hours, no more doing whatever you want, no more peanut butter and jelly sandwiches"... I swore to the straight and narrow right then and there. We were allowed to keep our bikes, with the stipulation of a parental phone call to the Sheriff. The next day, I fessed up with great trepidation, only to have my Dad laugh about it. He had grown up with the "arresting" Deputy, and that fact seemed to amuse him.

However, I did lose all camping and biking privileges for quite a while. I guess Dad wasn't totally amused. That was a gut wrenching, heart pounding event for sure!

Mornings in camp we would wake up bleary-eyed and wait for the dew to dry off the tent so we could tear it all down and move it off of our prized wiffle ball field, complete with twine outfield fencing and cardboard distance signs. We did need to know how far our latest homerun blast traveled! We cleared the field until the next campout. After all, the game must go on! Most days in the summer Larry and I would play homerun derby, or as many as seven guys from the neighborhood would divide into teams and the game was on. Most of us were on the same little league team, but wiffle ball was our off-day game. Dad never minded the grassless baselines in our yard, there is a man who understood priorities!

Dad took us brothers to the woods hunting morel mushrooms in the spring. Our older brother, Bob, went along on these forays. He was three years older than me, thus, he tended to hang with his "mature" friends most of the time. Mushroom hunting... that was different, he tolerated Larry and I for mushroom hunting. We walked for miles, heads down, hot on the trail. We never found many, but what a great time in the woods!

Many years later in life, Bob got permission to hunt mushrooms on a property in southern Ohio that he had helped survey a couple years earlier. Now Bob had become a pretty good finder of those tasty, fungus morsels and he graciously passed along closely guarded "shroomer" secrets. For several years we hiked those hills every spring in search of dining Nirvana. Father, sons, grandchildren, canteens, packs, walking sticks, all made for eagerly awaited spring, woods outings! That was hiking with a purpose. Those were good times indeed! I truly miss those outings.

I remember my last adolescent camp adventure. Three good friends, Steve, Mark, and Doug (all Boy Scouts and thus much more knowledgeable on gear and camping in general) and I planned a trip to Steve's grandmother's property about an hour south of our hometown. Now his grandmother lived in the hill country of Holmes County Ohio. She lived on top of a knoll in an old homestead house, still lacking electricity, if my memory serves me correctly. She was born, raised and, I guess, wanted to stay in those times. It was May and we were about to graduate from high school. The weather was cool but not too cold. We camped under the stars, roasting steaks and potatoes over an open fire. It couldn't get much better than that!

That night we visited the local VFW (Veterans of Foreign Wars) pond to fish and go for a swim. Northeast Ohio pond water in May, makes for an invigorating (read as: FREEZING COLD) experience. But we swam anyway just to prove to ourselves that we could. I would use that same flawed reasoning to justify many of my questionable exploits throughout my life. Still do to this day! Go figure.

The next day Steve led us through the woods searching for an old family coal mine. After 30 minutes of combing the woods, Steve proudly pointed to a three foot wide hole under a large boulder. Steve was the first to squeeze into the small opening under that boulder, down into the shaft. The tunnel dropped a few feet before it leveled out to horizontal, and led straight north into the hill. Determining all was safe, we planned our descent into the unknown. We decided, with good sense I might add, to leave two adventurers outside to go for help in case of a catastrophic cave-in. Steve and Mark became the safety sentinels, and waited outside as Doug and I headed in, flashlights in hand.

I, for no known reason, took the lead. A small room opened up immediately on the right. It was roughly 8-foot by 6-foot with a 7-foot ceiling. I was in awe considering its hand dug origins. Small fruit bats hung from the ceiling, adding to the mysterious aura of the tunnel. No wooden shoring was evident. The rock seemed to be secure and stable on its own. I was amazed at this first hand view of, a more "hands on", human existence. Man, a natural gas furnace suddenly took on a new sense of wonder!

About 25-feet in, a secondary shaft led off to the left but had standing water. As we continued on, the main shaft became smaller and smaller. Adventure and exploration overcame my very strong claustrophobic tendencies...well, for about 150-feet or so, anyway. At that point I was compactly crouched with my head bent forward as far as possible, yet it still touched the ceiling, and my knees contacted my chest. Panic ensued! I hyper-ventilated feeling that I would never see the light of day again. An ever-tightening constriction consumed me. Trapped! Maybe the opening had collapsed! Maybe we couldn't get out! I now had a human roadblock baring my retreat! I am ashamed to say, fear and dread were in total control. "Get the hell out of my way! ... GETTHEHELLOUTOFMYWAY !" I screamed, consumed with uncontrollable horror.

Doug, seemed to immediately grasp the seriousness of the situation, urged into action by my wild violent rants, he contorted into reverse position, and hurriedly backtracked the way we came, while being shoved the whole way by yours truly. Thank God, the small but welcoming hole to freedom was still there! Out to fresh air, open skies, and slow to come, normalized heart beats. I gladly tended to my safety watch while Steve and Mark ensued on their own explorations of the chasm. To this day, I leave spelunking to others!

You get the picture. That's how I roughed it, in the days of my youth. A well schooled man of the woods I was not.

Chapter 2

The Room of the Tell-Tale Heart - The Stuff Dreams are Made of

Fast forward to 1987. We were busy working, raising families and doing a little fishing in Northeast Ohio. We being myself and coworker Bob Weyandt. We worked in a small asphalt coatings manufacturing and packaging facility where we produced striping paints, patching materials, and tennis court coatings. The work was physical, hot, and summer-seasonal.

"Look at this article, Bob! That is where we need to go! Just look at those clear mountain streams, and the article says they are full of trout!" We read that article in an outdoor magazine, and began to map and plan a fall adventure to The Great Smoky Mountain National Park and surrounding areas. The trip would include some backpacking and stream fishing, both new to me. We would be off and casting as soon as things slowed down at work in the fall! Well, that season stretched on for what seemed like forever. We were chomping at the bit, when we thought we finally saw the end in sight, and a chance for our dream adventure in early October.

Bob, had been out west in the early 1970s. He saw Evel Knievel's Snake River Canyon Jump in Twin Falls, Idaho in '74. He hiked and camped the mountains of Colorado with an old high school buddy. He told us fellow workers, of those and other outdoor adventures, at lunch breaks, over Ho Hos and Ramen noodles.

Having never been hiking or backpacking in the mountains myself, I had preparations to address, state of the art gear and provisions to buy! Having very little money, and absolutely no practical knowledge of the needs such a trip might demand, I defaulted to my superior intuition. After all...I had watched the movie, *The Treasure of the Sierra Madre,* and I did end up with similar equipment...minus the burros! I'll explain more on my gear as the trip unfolds.

Well, our busy season stretched on...and on...and on, until we were thinking it would be too late in the year to go! Panic and disappointment were setting in. The trip of a lifetime was fading. Fall was slipping away and winter creeping ever closer. Finally, business slowed to a halt as October ended. The first week of November was launch time! We loaded up my Dodge Minivan (yes I had one of those), and hit the road. Great Smoky Mountains, here we come!

The last time I was...wait...the only time I was on a long road trip adventure with anyone but family, was eleven years earlier, the day after high school graduation. Two buddies and I drove 700 miles north to Gogama, Ontario in Canada. We stayed in a cabin on a fairly remote lake for a week. A small boat, great water, sweet little cabin, three 18-year-olds and Canadian beer! The stuff dreams are made of (minus beautiful Canadian girls). But, that's a story for another time.

I was overcome with the excitement and anticipation of the moment! Figuring if we left Wooster, Ohio at around 5PM, we would be at our first destination early the next morning. Our target was Dandridge, Tennessee and Douglas Lake. Douglas lake is a 300,000 acre 43-mile-long impoundment of the French Broad River, and one of the large jewels in the Tennessee Valley Authority's (TVA) crown. We pulled out of my driveway right on time and pointed that "Outdoorsman's Super Bus" south. The adventure was really happening!

Heading south on I77, I was on a mission, feeling, I'm sure, quite like the Knights Templar did the first time they rode out on the Great Crusade! Ok, maybe slightly less important as world events go, but I was overwhelmed to be underway just the same. Always one to be prepared, Bob had an ice chest between the front seats, filled with sandwiches, cokes, candy bars and everything else two explorers might need to climb Everest! After an exhausting 30 miles or so, Bob opened the magic vault between us, keen for an energy lift.

"Candy bar?" he asked. I looked over to see myriad of possible choices.

Holy Cow... Hershey and Nestle would be proud of his inventory. So much chocolate and so few days to consume it! That was Bob, always prepared and always ready for chocolate. A Mars Bar comfortably filled my hand as I continued my pilot's duties. Life was good..

Energy levels renewed, we traveled on for about 50 more miles. Coming to Marietta and the Ohio River, we spotted a sight too captivating to pass up. The Golden Arches called to us and we listened.

With my usual order in those days, I drove across the Ohio River into West Virginia. Almost heaven, with 2 Big Macs, large fries, and a coke in my possession. Yeah... yeah, I know, but it was 1987 and I considered that to be a normal meal at the time. Doesn't make it right, just the way it was. So we continued on at 65 mph winding through the mountains, contented and full.

I can't remember exactly where we were in West Virginia, somewhere along the turn-pike, when we noticed these really cool looking lights lining the mountainside along the left side of the highway.

"What the hell are those lights?" I asked Bob. "Looks really cool." It was as if someone had strung twinkling, amber lights, for miles along the hillsides.

He wasn't sure what we were seeing either. Then we smelled smoke. Damn, the mountains were on fire! And it was getting very close to the highway! The smoke was gathering in the low area, which was the roadbed! It was an unbelievable sight. Beautiful really, but terrifying at the same time. We were beginning to worry about getting through this inferno. For several miles the forest on the east side of the highway was burning, and at times we could see flames leaping 40 feet or more into the air above the trees. In a few places, both sides of the highway were engulfed. The whole thing was quite concerning indeed! I don't recall seeing much in the way of emergency vehicles, and there were no warnings at all. We left it all behind after about 20 miles. We were a bit shaken but none the worse for wear, with a new experience under our belts. I believe I later read that over 400,000 acres burned in that wildfire. I don't want to see another one. But, since it happened and we suffered no negative effects, I am thankful for the experience .

Somewhere around 25 miles from Dandridge we saw a sign for Crockett's Tavern in Morristown, Tennessee. It was 1:30 in the morning, and we figured a 25- mile detour (50mi round trip) wouldn't hurt a thing. We were both suckers for old historic buildings, besides, we were talking about a piece of Davy's history, or so we thought. It was a no-brainer, a sure thing for a guy with no brains, right? Following the signs, we pulled into the gravel parking lot around 2am. Probably not the smartest thing to do, we jumped out of our "DeLorean"... and back in time! I know, I know.. a bad reference to the movie, *Back to the Future*. I couldn't help myself.

Anyway, not knowing the tavern was built as a museum in 1950's, to commemorate and obviously capitalize on Davy Crockett's legend, we skulked around the two story, flat hewn log, structure, with flashlights in hand, giddy as a couple school kids, amazed at the old implements of the time period, visible through the windows. We could see a large stone fireplace, complete with hanging cast iron cooking pots, a spinning wheel, butter churn, plates, cups, and other utensils of the time. Many candle holders and lanterns graced the tables and log walls. We made a quick tour around the structure, taking in all possible views. Relieved that no police officers showed up to assist with our museum tour, we returned to 1987 and headed back toward the small town of Dandridge and Douglas Lake, past history securely tucked under our belts.

The night ebbed from fairly clear with moonlight illuminating our view, to being slightly obscured by settling fog. Crossing a bridge, we caught our first glimpse of Douglas lake. What the heck, the lake was drying up! The water level was so low that at places, it was 100 yards or more from the original shoreline to the water's edge! It looked like we were approaching an alien planet. We looked at each other ...Oh, this looked like great planning. Not quite sure what tomorrow would bring, we drove around looking for somewhere to pull over, gather our thoughts, and possibly get some sleep. A broad pull-off on the right side of the road served our purpose. We were both worried about the water level of the lake. We each had a ham sandwich and a coke while pondering tomorrow's plan. Fatigue settling in, we brushed our teeth using water from our army surplus canteens...well we were civilized, you know. With the temperature dropping, we each sat in our front seats, covered up with our sleeping bags. Sleep came quickly.

We got a couple hours of much needed sleep before awakening to dense fog and temperatures in the mid 30's. It was just getting light, and we were eager to get a closer look at lake conditions. Finding a point of access, we climbed out and headed toward the shoreline. Damn... it was cold! Sure enough you could walk, on what was previously lakebed. How could we not know this lake was drying up? Disappointment aside, it was pretty cool checking out logs, rocks, tires, dead fish and the occasional engine block lying on the exposed lakebed. It was like a treasure trove. We spent most of the day checking out the lake.

Thank God! The lake was not drying up! We talked to a convenience store clerk, and found out the TVA drops water levels by as much as 40-feet after the summer season, for power generation, and flood control purposes. Being used to fishing our local waters, such as 63 acre Shreve Lake, and 107- acre Odell Lake, 43-mile-long, 300,000-acre Douglas Lake was totally foreign and spectacular to us. My excitement was building, and I couldn't wait to fish this monster!

I had made reservations at a quaint (read as: questionable), inexpensive lake side motel complete with two bedrooms and a full kitchen. I'll call it Snag Bay Motel and General Store (fictitious). I couldn't tell you if the place still exists or not. The owners, Tom and his wife Deb (names changed to protect the privacy of a wonderful couple), were very nice people. Originally from up north, we had some commonality with them, and we got along great. The room fit our needs just fine, but we never could quite figure what the rather strange, obtrusive odor was. We joked about the "dead guy" under the floor boards. That was probably the only time Bob didn't really mind my lighting up a cigar, which I did at times in those days. The aroma of cigar smoke was a dubious improvement. Overlooking that, we enjoyed our short-term home.

Evening came and we bought some worms for bait at the store. Deb could not believe we wanted to fish that night.

"It's going to get really cold tonight, you don't want to be out there," she insisted.

"We are from Northeastern Ohio and we came to fish," Bob assured her, insinuating our extreme outdoorsman's prowess and toughness.

With a look of, "Oh Brother" plastered on her face, she pointed out some lawn chairs and the dock out back. She wished us "good luck" as we exited for the dock and fishing nirvana.

I sat there on the dock, with fishing rod in one hand, and a cup of coffee in the other, while Bob's Coleman, gas lantern hissed out hand warming light. We had it made, this was what we came for. We caught several 8 to 9- inch bass right away. Nothing to brag about, but these Ohio boys were gettin' after it! Shortly, we both had problems reeling in line. Upon further inspection, we found our wet, line was freezing up solid at our tip guides. We would hold our rod tips close to the lantern long enough to thaw things, then cast again. I guess Deb was right, it was pretty cold. By 10:00, our fishing appetite satisfied for the night, we headed for a good night's sleep, over top of our roommate, "the dead guy".

The morning dawned cloudy, windy, and cool. We asked Tom for a boat to rent, and he informed us there wasn't a boat for rent on the lake this time of year. But, we pleaded that it was supposed to be a decent day, and we were there to fish. After some prodding from his wife, Tom pulled a motor out of winter storage, mounted it on a 12-foot aluminum boat, and sent us on our way. Now, that might tell you what a fine couple they were.

We fished several coves and explored as much of the lake as we could that day. A fine day on the lake and enough fish to fry for dinner was our reward! Thanks to Tom and Deb, we had a great stay on Douglas Lake. But we had places to go and things to do, it was time to move on.

Driving through Pigeon Forge towards Gatlinburg, and the looming Smoky Mountains...that was a magic moment in my life. The awe, excitement, and anticipation were overwhelming. I hadn't actually walked on, or touched mountains since I was in the Rocky Mountains on family vacation when I was ten. And I loved the mountains then. Knowing I was going to be in the historic, ancient Smokies, actually hiking through them, I was so excited that I could hardly stand it!

Gatlinburg was narrow streets winding through antique, craft and art shops, restaurants, hotels, and other tourist attractions. We wound through town noting anything of interest for later possible investigation. There was a beautiful, rushing mountain stream winding along the road on our right, as we drove through town. We envisioned trout behind every rock in that beckoning water! With no time to linger, we continued toward the Sugarlands Visitor Center, the north central entrance of the Smokies.

My heart was racing as we pulled off route 441 to take the obligatory photos with the Great Smoky Mountain National Park "welcome sign" behind us. Wow, how could I have lived just a few hundred miles from this beautiful wilderness and never been there? I could see, feel, smell this wonderful (new to me) paradise. Soon we would be... in it...experiencing it...a part of it. I can't explain it to this day. Thirty some years later I can tell you, the Blue Ridge Mountains and especially the Smokies, grabbed hold of me that day, and still refuse to let go.

The Sugarlands Visitor Center is a must for anyone heading into the park for the first time. I don't know how many times I have been there, but I can tell you I still look forward to a stop there whenever I can. And, as you will find out, my visits to the Smokies are a favorite pastime. After some well spent time gathering information and trail maps at the visitor center, we were on the way to the Elkmont camping area.

Once in the Elkmont camping area, we watched a well equipped fisherman walk up stream toward the bridge where we stood. I inquired as to his luck. The hip-booted angler opened his creel, revealing four very nice trout! "It takes nothing special," he assured us. "move slowly and hit the deeper pools behind larger rocks," the expert instructed. I Thanked him for his advice and we hurried over to set up our camp, before hitting the stream with the express intent of gathering dinner!

Bright sun, warm, calm weather, and clear rushing mountain water, what a day. It could not get much better! Off we went casting and retrieving with our small spinning outfits and telescoping rods. Man, we were living the dream. An entire afternoon of nothing but fishing- heaven, in the Smokies.

We were quite disappointed when both of us returned to camp empty handed. Maybe there was a learning curve we hadn't counted on. Well, Campbell's soup heated on our Coleman two burner camp stove, along with bologna sandwiches tasted pretty darn good anyway. We discussed tomorrow's foray into the world of backcountry camping. The heck with fishing, we had a whole lot of forested mountains to explore.

The next morning, standing beside the sign for Jakes Creek Trail, I had the same kind of feeling as the first time I strapped on catchers' equipment for a little league baseball game. Donning that equipment felt really special. Ready to crouch behind home plate, but very nervous about getting it done without embarrassing myself. With a similar nervousness, I hitched up all the gear needed for a night in the back country, for the very first time. I felt like that kid again.

I must have been an impressive sight as we started up the trail toward campsite #27 (Lower Jakes Gap). I fully admit to having had no idea of modern hiking/camping gear. Of course, being slight on funds limited any thoughts of real equipment anyway.

Now I ask you to close your eyes and picture me at that moment... An adjustable ball cap with mesh vented panels for ventilation topped my head. Aviator sunglasses, of course, shielded my eyes. Cotton pocket t-shirt and blue jeans protected my torso. A sturdy bright orange nylon book bag/ruck sack, complete with fake leather hard plastic bottom and lash tabs carried my essentials. Tent and poles were lashed to the top flap of my pack, and an army surplus sleeping bag lashed to the bottom. For cooking purposes, a full, two- quart blanket canteen was lashed on the back. For my base I wore very comfortable tennis shoes.

We both carried large sheath knives and WWII army surplus canteens on our belts. Bob did have a 1970s frame pack (yes, a real pack) and heavy leather hiking boots. He carried the two burner Coleman camp stove in one hand and a Coleman single mantle lantern in the other. I carried the can of white gas for refueling in one hand and a 6-pack cooler to ensure the freshness of refrigerated meat and chocolate in the other hand. High Tech! And speaking only for myself, I carried several extra pounds of stomach in front of me. OK... open your eyes and try to erase that ugly vision from your memory as quick as you can! Unfortunately, it is permanently burned into mine, never to be erased.

Jakes Creek Trail starts at an elevation of around 2300' and steadily climbs for about 2.5 miles before reaching camp #27 (Lower Jakes Gap) at 3520'. Nice forest and a stream made for a pleasant setting indeed. I astutely noticed two things that day. Number one - I was not in great shape and climbing 1200' in 2.5 miles with a sagging 50 pounds hanging off my back, was quite taxing. Second - Even though Bob was a few years older than me, and therefore in my eyes somewhat worse off than I envisioned myself, he could trudge steadily onward and upward when I needed to pause for rest and water. That trend continued for several more years. Anyway, perceptions can be deceiving. We finally reached #27 and dropped our gear for a well-deserved rest.

While eating a little granola, downing some water, and checking the map, we noticed a little further up the trail at Jake's Gap, there was a short side trail climbing to the top of Blanket Mountain....might as well. We hit the trail, carrying canteens only, after stashing our packs behind some thick laurel. With lighter loads and attitudes, we climbed just under a mile to the end of the trail at Jake's Gap (elevation 4,055'). Here, we could choose Miry Ridge Trail, Panther Creek Trail or the trail up Blanket Mountain. So many ways through these mountains. I wanted to trek them all.

The trail itself was a bit overgrown, and climbed roughly 500 feet in elevation in about 3/4 of a mile, terminating at the summit. Part way up, there was a rock outcrop with some great views of surrounding mountain peaks and a nice open valley which we would later found to be Cades Cove.

Cades Cove is an extremely interesting example of Appalachian history. The cove was originally settled by John and Lucretia Oliver and their infant daughter, in the fall of 1818, with only Cherokee Indians as distant neighbors. A Tenuous situation for a lone family. Interestingly, the story says that they would have surely starved that first lonely winter if not for the Cherokees leaving dried pumpkin for the "white" settlers. They continued as the lone settlers until 1821 when a few others followed their lead. The "original" Oliver cabin (I'll explain later), still stands today. In fact, an 11-mile loop road runs through the cove where you can visit homestead cabins, out buildings, churches, cemeteries and more. The cove is a well-preserved and compelling slice of early American mountain life.

We were disappointed to find views very limited once we reached the summit due to trees and brush. There are still remnants of the concrete base of a long gone fire tower. As always, relics of the past were really exciting to see. We searched for awhile, but found very little evidence of previous activities. Overall, Blanket Mountain was an enjoyable side trip.

Site #27, was large enough for around eight people and horses. We set up in the back end of the camping area in order to insulate our camp from any late arrivals. Our tent was an inexpensive, 3- man, dome tent, with 2 shock corded fiberglass poles. When my brother Bob heard about my planned trip, he offered the tent for our use. He had set it up in his yard for his kids to play in. It worked great and we would stay dry he assured. This was free housing, and quite different from the last tent I had camped in (remember that 300# army surplus tent in our back yard). Once the tent was erected, we threw in our sleeping bags and headed to the communal fire pit with our stove, lantern, and packs in hand, equipped for dinner prep. It would be on a rainy night several days later that I would find out modern tents were also supposed to have an attachable rain fly. I'm slow on the uptake.

Just imagine two burners going, one for coffee/tea water, and on the other, a can of vegetable soup with added hot dogs for needed protein. All cooking in Bob's army surplus mess kit pan. That's what backpacker dreams are made of! Am I right, or what? While the stove did its work, we each had a Hostess Ho Ho for an appetizer. Two guys of the woods, home on our backs, self reliant, and living the dream! So this was what it's all about. We were loving life on the trail.

A hot beverage in one hand and a desert candy bar in the other, we were relaxing against a log when the rustling sound and heavy footsteps from up the trail, caught our attention. Expecting a bear to rip the candy bar from my grasp, I thought..."from my cold dead hand." Too dramatic? No doubt, I guess I'm getting carried away. Anyway, out of the advancing dusk, stumbled an extremely tired, huffing, puffing, fellow hiker.

Exchanging pleasantries of the trail, we invited our new-found friend, Ray, to share in our dining bounty. His eyes and demeanor brightened considerably upon seeing our candy bars. After listing to the menu choices we could offer, Ray eagerly accepted a ham sandwich, a Ho Ho and some Snack Pack pudding. After many days of dehydrated pack food, he was elated to partake in our offerings. See, I told you.... the stuff dreams are made of!

Poor Ray, his wife had left him six months ago back in Texas. He left Texas, and had been traveling, hiking, and camping, to clear his head ever since. The last 3 weeks had been spent in the Smokies. We traded hiking stories for awhile, then he passed out where he had collapsed. We gathered our gear headed back to our tent.

It was a clear night and we fell asleep enjoying the starry sky through our mesh ceiling. Being November, most of the trees had dropped their leaves giving us a fairly unobstructed view. The sound of movement and crunching from all around us woke me at 3am. I woke Bob who was happily snoring in deep slumber. Grabbing flashlights, we unzipped the tent door and peered into the darkness. Glowing eyes met our illuminating beams. There were 15 sets of deer eyes looking our way. They paid little attention to us as they munched their late night meal. That solidified it, we were one with nature. It didn't take long for the crunching to succumb to our renewed snoring.

After a coffee and Ho Ho breakfast, we bid farewell to Ray and broke camp to return to our trusty minivan. The realization that I was now a true man of the trail gave me great confidence and enthusiasm. We cheerily hailed every hiker heading up the trail with the knowledge of where they were headed. Been there... Done that.

In camp we had decided to leave the Jake's Gap area for higher ground. We wanted to get to the top. We were off to Clingmans Dome!

At 6643', Clingmans Dome is the 3rd highest peak east of the Mississippi River. All three peaks are within about 100 miles of each other. Mount Mitchell (6684'), and

Mount Craig (6647'), are the only peaks higher Clingmans Dome. Clingmans is the highest point within the Great Smoky Mountains National Park, and the highest point on the over 2180-mile Appalachian Trail. With a paved 7-mile access road and an observation tower on the peak, it is a popular tourist spot.

We stopped at Elkmont to complete a new back country camping permit before driving the 27- mile winding road to the Dome. What a road it is, winding, circling, with switch backs, pull offs, and fabulous overlooks, the road itself is an adventure worth the trip. I think we stopped at every overlook, including Newfound Gap, where the road crests and heads down and into Cherokee, North Carolina.

Leaving Route 441, we drove the 7-mile road to Clingmans Dome. Man, we were going to take on one of the highest peaks in the eastern U.S.! Well, we were going to start there anyway. Being a flatlander, the elevation did cause some apprehension. Thin air? Oh, I take in a lot of oxygen. I hoped that would not be a problem. The road wound continually up and up. The morning was cool with a constant breeze. We were in heavy fog as we entered the parking lot. There were several cars and a group bus parked, and people milled about the area.

We headed up the 1/2-mile paved walkway leading to the observation tower. The tower itself is a curving concrete ramp terminating with a round observation platform atop the 54' structure. 360-degree views of the surrounding mountains and valleys, including Fontana Lake, awaited our arrival, if not for the enveloping fog. Disappointment from the lack of vision failed to dampen our enthusiasm for the trek across the top of the Smokies. A stop at the restrooms near the parking lot assured our trail readiness as well as full canteens.

I invite you to envision our mountain rain gear (a light misty rain was falling) added to the previously described packing garb. Mine, being an inexpensive bright yellow plastic coat, complete with plastic snaps, and pant ensemble. It surely enhanced my credibility as a well-prepared mountain trekker. You might picture me in a bright yellow garbage bag pant suit. I'm certain you can envision that. Damn it...I can.

We proudly strutted back up the paved walkway, with assured confidence that our presence was noted by all of the typical "day" tourists, with great respect and admiration. We were truly on a different level, ready to travel the backbone of this 480-million-year-old mountain system!

Our plan was to head west on the legendary Appalachian Trail, following the ridgeline approximately 2.5 miles, to our camp for the night. This trail promised narrow ridges that offer beautiful views of valleys, ridges, mountains, and towns, miles away. We could envision all of this along with the picturesque high-country camp named Double Spring Gap. I imagined a mountain meadow with two cascading water sources and readymade shelter big enough for twelve. This could once again be, the stuff dreams are made of!

Stepping off into the misty fog, we entered the revered Appalachian Trail. Wow, I couldn't believe I was on one of the most famous trails in the country, probably the world! I was completely awestruck as we came onto a narrow rock ridgeline, just as the fog cleared away enough to allow a view of several side ridges and peaks to the north. Narrow and rocky, my right foot was in Tennessee and my left in North Carolina, very cool indeed. We took our good old time and enjoyed every minute of this relatively short hike. Starting at over 6600', we descended with only one real climb as we topped Mount Buckley, before reaching our destination at around 5500'.

The stuff dreams are made of? The entire area around the shelter was littered with empty booze bottles, food packaging, and bits of toilet paper. Even a pile of puke was visible by a log about 20' from the shelter. Oh my God...what a mess of a disappointment. Even the fireplace within the shelter held bottles and foil packaging. What kind of morons come out here just to defile the beauty of nature? I have since come to realize, a close proximity to vehicle access, brings weekend party goers to otherwise great natural areas. Damn shame.

We cleaned up as much as we could and bagged what we thought we could carry out. We now felt as if we could make the shelter, our home for the night as originally intended.

The shelter itself had rock sides and back, with an open front facing the valley extending, I believe, to the west. I might explain later just how poor I am at judging direction. Anyway, the open front is actually enclosed by a chain link fence with a swinging door in the middle. At this point we could not quite figure out the reason for the fencing. Could be to keep bears out. Could be to keep drunken morons out. Either way, we guessed it could be useful. The 12 bunks consisted of wire mesh stretched between wooden frames.

As darkness descended, hot dogs and soup were prepared by flashlight. I can tell you it did taste darn good after our day of adventure, discovery and disappointment.

By now the temperature had dropped considerably and the wind was howling up the valley and directly into the shelter. Bob carried an army surplus arctic sleeping bag good, according to him, down to somewhere around 150 below zero. I believed him because it weighed about 1 pound for every degree of protection below zero! Damn, Bob could carry a lot of weight. That thing was very heavy. Anyway, he had given me use a lighter weight surplus bag that he had. I could carry it without compressing any vertebrae, so it was probably good to around plus 40. Gale force winds whipped through our protective chain link, rendering me mildly uncomfortable (read as: BONE CHILLINGLY COLD). Even as Bob assured me of the high quality of such military equipment, I whined like a puppy whose mother couldn't produce enough milk. I did not take it like a man.

Dreary, misty, dim morning light never looked so good. Hot coffee and oatmeal warmed and rejuvenated me. Packing our gear, we again donned rainwear. It was time to leave Double Spring Gap. This would be a place I would remember, however, not as fondly as I had hoped. I later read somewhere, that during the height of the '70s backpacking craze, several hundred campers all showed up at Double Spring...on the same night! That's the stuff nightmares are made of. Makes me cringe just thinking about it. Probably explains some of the crap we packed out.

Moving out, we each carried a garbage bag of trash from the site. I found my feet heavier, and breathing more labored on that morning. I'm not sure if it was due to lack of sleep, thinner air, or a little depression, due to the lack of personal responsibility we witnessed the previous night. I do know I came to the conclusion, that wearing tennis shoes was a major miscalculation. I was learning that trails made up of course, rough, pointy rocks were not the place to carry heavy loads while wearing soft soled shoes! Not the best decision I've ever made.

Stumbling out of the forest into the parking lot back at Clingmans Dome, I once again felt like a conquering hero returning from our personal commune with nature. We were conscious of the downright envious looks the others in the parking lot gave us. I have with later contemplation, wondered if those looks were actually envy? What the heck...we'll call it envy.

The weather was taking a turn for the worse, so we spent the night in a motel in Pigeon Forge. The motel was inexpensive and had the added luxury of a drive-thru office. We ordered a room and a six pack of beer. Very efficient. We awoke to four inches of fresh snow. The Mountains were beautiful, but I figured I would have frozen to death up there.

We spent a few more nights in the National Park's developed campgrounds, and explored a few more trails. We toured Cades Cove, and its many historic buildings. I did pick up some trail maps and a complete hiking trail guide book there. I knew they would come in handy later.

We caught no fish on the trail. Honestly, after leaving Douglas Lake, we never fished that much. We did visit and fish a little at Cherokee Lake, also in Tennessee, on the way back to Ohio. To finish the trip off with distinction, we were asked to leave Ohio's Salt Fork State Park at 3am, as we fished from a marina dock. The ranger accused us of sleeping, and therefore loitering. In reality he was very perceptive.

Overall, I had a great time. I learned a little about the workings of TVA lakes. We spent a couple nights with our "dead guy roommate", and we gleefully fished Douglas Lake. We touched, smelled, and walked the Great Smoky Mountains. We communed with fellow backpackers. We slept, surrounded by a herd of dining deer. We hiked on the acclaimed Appalachian Trail.

It was, after the fact, obvious to me, and now surely to you, that I really wasn't prepared, or even very knowledgeable about backpacking, backcountry camping, or mountain stream fishing. My gear was heavy, clumsy, and in many cases, downright inadequate, although, I did make it work for me. The added weight of improper gear and food made for unwanted extra exertion. Double Spring Gap revealed, that romantic visions of unknown trails and camps can be deceptive.

However, that trip was a big success. Bob was a great hiking companion and he willingly put up with all of my rookie mistakes and complaining. Best of all, I was introduced to one of my favorite natural places.

The fire had been lit.

Chapter 3
Naval Invasion, and the
"Skunk Whisperer"

Ever since that trip in '87 I was eager to commune with the backcountry again. My brother, Larry, and I had been giving the idea plenty of thought. Most things I've done were done with him - still are. We had been running a youth football program together since 1976, and any plans to hit the trail had to wait until November, after the finish of our season. Larry headed up the wheat breeding program at the Ohio Agricultural Research and Development Center (OARDC), and the harvest would be done, cataloged, and the next crop planted by then. We planned on an early November launch.

We were brewing a batch of ale as we had done so often since our first brew in the fall of 1982. This one was a nut brown ale, our first attempt at that particular style. The malt was in the kettle and we had just started the boil with addition number one of Kent Goldings hops. Kent Goldings added a spicy, somewhat floral smell to the chocolaty, roasted, coffeeish, malt, and steeping grains. The aroma was heavenly. Brewing sessions are perfect for discussing anything and everything from coaching strategies, to motorcycle trips, the Browns, the Indians, and now, backpacking. Nothing much better than brewing a beer, mulling over anything on our minds, while drinking a couple of bottled remnants from our last brewing session.

I laid a trail map of the Smokies on the dining room table. "Just look at all the trails on this map. Almost no roads and over 800 miles of backcountry trails!"

Research was under way. *Backpacker Magazine* was read in earnest. We sent for and perused mail order equipment catalogs. We hit the jackpot when we discovered Kames, an outdoor store in North Canton, Ohio.

Now we could see, touch, and feel what we were reading about! And oh, how we studied that trail guide and maps, I had purchased in Cades Cove two years earlier.

As before, money was an issue. I needed a pack. Yes, I decided to retire the orange book bag! A mid-sized Camp Trails external frame pack got my nod. While not a high-end choice, it was a huge improvement over "Old Orange". A couple Nalgene water bottles, and an aluminum cook pot along with utensils were next. A Coleman 30 degree sleeping bag with stuff sack was a big improvement over.....well, over nothing, which was what I owned previously. While we intended to carry quite a bit of water, I purchased a Sweet Water filter. Now we could use the available natural water sources safely. A Wenzel dome tent would provide our shelter. Mid top, light- weight hiking boots, completed my gear.

Larry went with a slightly smaller, Camp Trails external frame pack. He picked out a better choice of sleeping bag, a Slumberjack Hollowfill, and Merrell hiking boots would protect his feet. His pride and joy was a Swedish made, Optimus Svea 123 white gas backpack, camp stove. Very cool, reliable, but quirky piece of equipment.

We both chose RidgeRest closed cell foam sleeping pads for sleeping comfort and insulation from cold, wet ground.

We mapped and remapped loop trails which we felt we could complete in three or four days, while pouring over the trail maps and the detailed descriptions in the trail guide. With so many trails and different terrain choices, we studied the options endlessly. Down around Fontana lake, out of Deep Creek, Cades Cove, Cosby, Smokemont, Big Creek, Cataloochee, it was a lot to consider. We still find this process to be a most enjoyable part of each trip. The first trip for these two novice hikers would be special. With total disregard for the fact that Bob and I had done less than three miles under pack at any one time, Larry and I planned considerably longer days.

We nodded in agreement, satisfied with one particular route. Our planned trip would take us 33 miles in 4 days. Starting once again on Jake's Creek Trail, ever upward over the third highest peak in the eastern U.S., Clingmans Dome, then down around the other side, winding back to our starting point.

We would hike up steeply for seven miles the first day. Second day would be another taxing climb up and over Clingmans Dome and down the other side for a 14-mile day. A mild 7.7- mile third day. Fourth day, a cake walk of a day at four miles. We would see it all - Rivers, streams, high ridge views, deep forests, hills, balds, valleys, and "The Dome"! Our homes and life sustaining provisions all on our backs. Both of us, one with the mountains and on our own hook.

What the hell were we thinking?

Saturday November 4, 10PM, we were on our way, and it was so exciting! Our equipment was stashed in the back of my 1981 Ford Mustang 2- door. Powerful, it was not... fast, it was not... luxurious, it was not... taking us to "The Promised Land", it most certainly was! We were off, down I75 with nothing to do but, discuss life, and anticipated life on the trail. A few cups of coffee and a sandwich or two had us clicking off the miles with ease. Passing the decorative Ferris wheel while topping Jellico Mountain in Tennessee, we could feel our destination on the horizon. About two hours later we were driving through Knoxville and saying goodbye to I75. Taking Route 441 into Pigeon Forge, we made our way to the Sugarlands Visitor Center. While not open at 6AM, the center had very nice restrooms, just the place for our comfort and trail preparations. It was the perfect stop after driving all night, and before hitting the trail for the day. Canteens and water bottles were filled for the coming trek.

Feeling somewhat refreshed, we drove on to Elkmont campground. We filled out our backcountry registration and attached the designated tag to my pack before advancing to the trailhead.

Fog loomed at the trailhead, as the very first hint of the approaching daylight faintly illuminated our surroundings. Both of us attempted to stretch out the kinks from the trip. We changed socks, laced up our hiking shoes, and lashed our outer gear to our packs. Being a little unsure of the water sources in the higher elevations, we each carried around ten pounds of water. All tolled, we each hoisted very close to 60 pounds of shiny new equipment onto our backs. I felt much better prepared than I was on my first attempt.

Stepping onto the trail at about 2300' of elevation, our bodies were somewhat hesitant, considering over eight hours of sitting in the car, the newness of backpacking in its own right, and the ample added weight. Before long, we walked into a steady rhythm. We stopped for a break at my previous one night's domain, campsite #27. Larry got an ear full of my first visit to that hallowed ground.

I was feeling the effects of driving all night, and hoisting the heavy load. After all we both had been going since around 6 AM the previous day. By the time we reached Jakes Gap, the 1700' - 3.3-mile climb had wreaked havoc on both my ability and desire to continue any further. Spreading my blue tarp/ground cloth out on the gap's forest floor, at the foot of Blanket Mountain, I laid my head on my pack and reclined, for a needed rest. Larry decided to follow my lead. I awoke from a sound sleep to find Larry talking to four middle- aged women who were looking my way as if they had spotted a bear just off the trail. I rose to pay the fellow hikers my respects. Those four regularly gathered two times a week to day hike the park's trails. It was obvious, as they headed up Blanket Mountain, that they could get it done. Larry then laughingly explained that my ferocious snoring had alerted them to this slumbering trailside "bear"! It couldn't have been that bad.

Feeling better rested, we hid our gear and hiked up Blanket Mountain. I was anxious to share this quick side trip with Larry. After appreciating the views and "bareback" walk, we re-shouldered our packs and pressed on.

Only 2.3 more miles on Miry Ridge Trail would put us at camp #26, (Dripping Springs). The trail, at times, lived up to its name. Slippery and downright muddy! It steadily climbed around 600' in 1.5 miles. At one point we looked back to see Blanket Mountain rising a few miles behind us. That was the first time we could look back over the miles we had hiked just hours before. That was really cool.

It was about then that a disturbing proclivity exposed itself from deep within Larry's darkest cranial reaches. Swear to God, he suddenly let loose with his best karaoke version of Billy Joel's *We didn't Start the fire.* The song had just been released and I hadn't heard it before.

"What the hell is that," I blurted in protest.

"It's Billy Joel's new song, I can't get it out of my head," he almost apologized.

A few minutes later he was at it again. I made fun of him once more, and he pleaded stupidity. This strange, one song musical "possession" repeated itself often on the entire four day trip. Future trips would bring out the same disturbing activity. Same weird unintentional jam session except, a different song. I feel an oncoming slander suit over exposing this debacle. Larry, I could not give you a pass on this one. To this day he says he remembers no such occurrences. I wish I could wipe it from my memory that easily.

Down we descended, onto a narrow, wooded ridge, and into camp #26 (Dripping Springs), home for the night!

It was mid-afternoon, which gave us some time to set camp, relax, and recover. Setting camp was all new to us. You would never have known. I can't explain it, we just went about setting up as if we had a plan and pre-designated chores. We had never discussed or even thought about it ahead of time, it just happened (has continued that way ever since).

This narrow ridge offered very nice views of mountains, valleys, and ridges off to the east. Views to the west were obstructed by trees which offered some protection from any winds blowing from that direction. We were surprised to find a rather large fire pit and chunked firewood just over the ridge behind us.

That night we prepared our first trail meal of dehydrated beef stew and coffee, on Larry's Svea. Now, if you have never used a Svea, it is an event all its own. After placing a little fuel in a depression (cup) around the fuel delivery tube, you light the fuel and let it burn in order to warm the fuel delivery tube. Once the tube is warmed, you open the fuel valve. Warning...this operation may lead to a rather high flame for a short time! Once the warming is complete, the stove settles into a very distinct sputtering flame. That sputtering sound comes to me even now as I write this.

We decided to have a fire, once the food bag was hung over a high tree limb in order to discourage any nearby bears. The large, safe looking pit and pre-cut wood led us to this decision. We had a nice fire going and were laughing about my earlier "bear growl" snoring, when four deer walked right up near the other side of the fire and watched us intently for several minutes. That was a fitting end to our very first ever, day on the trail. We had been up and functioning for over 36 hours straight (forgetting the Jakes Gap nap). Thoroughly dousing the fire, an absolute must every time, we retired for the night. It had been a good day.

Morning broke clear and beautiful. Larry fired the Svea for Oatmeal and coffee preparation. We both found standing and moving to be a chore. It felt like I was in *The Wizard of Oz,* and I was the Tin Man, before Dorothy applied much needed oil to my stiff rusty joints. My God...what happened to the points of my hips. They felt as if a small, camp "bone mason", had been hammering and chiseling on them with his little tools all night! Amazingly, Larry had the exact same malady.

We both found cinching the hip belts of our packs to be agonizingly painful, and we broke camp believing neither one of us could stand the hip torture for long. We even considered spending another day at #26, before we vowed to quit whining and hit the trail. That day was to be a 14-mile ordeal. Oh ya...and we were supposed to climb straight over 6643' Clingmans Dome! That was to be a 2200' gain in elevation. Again...what were we thinking!

It was quite evident early on, that the day would be a true test of our mental fortitude as well as our physical abilities. Shortly after getting started, rounding a bend, we were staring at a steep rise. The terrain had gotten in my head. That damn rise actually angered me. Why couldn't the trail just be flat? I didn't want to go up anymore. Three steps then rest...three steps then rest. This pattern continued until I reached the top. It wasn't a long climb, just fairly steep. I collapsed, unable to make my legs move. Larry came back and sat down.

"My legs are rubber." I whined.

"Just let them rest. They will recover." Larry assured me.

I know what was going through his mind. "Climbing Clingmans Dome with this loser, great idea."

I finally got to my feet after about twenty minutes. Off we went. The trail flattened out and things felt better. We were actually enjoying the nice, flat section of trail, when Larry spotted a large wire cage (trap), with its door open, in it's up position, ready to slam shut on the intended predator. We figured it to be meant for a vicious, rogue, problem bear. We continued up the trail, thinking it was cool to be in the wild, with large predators close at hand. Nearing a bend in the trail, we heard a deep menacing growl, close by just around the bend, and possibly on the hillside above us. We looked at each other, wondering just what we were approaching (we were both thinking bear), and after seeing the cage, a nasty bear, for sure. Our options were, turn back, or cautiously move forward, hoping for the best. I pulled my sheath knife as we stepped forward.

"I suppose you think you are going to "Daniel Boone it", and fight off a big mean bear with that," Larry looked amused.

"No, if it attacks, I'm going to use this to slit your throat, leave you as a distraction, and run like hell." We both laughed, and slowly continued onward. I can tell we were nervous for the next 1/2-mile or so. Whatever it was, it sounded very large, and quite unwelcoming. We never did find out what we heard, and we were pretty ok with that.

The next trail sign lightened our mood -
Appalachian Trail (AT)....Silers Bald 2.9 miles- We were
on the AT. The trail gained 500' in elevation, climbing to
the bald. We trudged 2.9 miles. Just before the bald, there
was an AT shelter for overnight stays. It was typical with
three rock walls and a chain link fence protecting the open
front. We rested, ate a quick lunch, and paid tribute to our
progress.

From the shelter, we started up the trail toward the bald,
and ultimately, Clingmans Dome. After a quarter of a mile
and a 200' climb, we reached the bald. Silers Bald is a
5600' grassy meadow with some decent views of distant
peaks. This bald was not being maintained by the Park
Service (per *Hiking Trails of the Smokies* by Great Smoky
Mountains Natural History Association), and some trees
and vegetation were starting to overtake the bald.

While no one is quite sure what caused the grassy balds
(20 grassy balds in the Park- GreatSmokies.net), It is
generally believed that pasturing cattle on these high points
in the summer, kept trees and brush from advancing on
them, leaving open grassy meadows. It is noted, (*Cades
Cove-The Life And Death Of A Southern Appalachian
Community 1818-1937* by Durwood Dunn) that the
presence of some of the balds before white settlement, was

recorded in Cherokee legend. On the other hand, records of Cades Cove indicate that they are not natural. John W. Oliver stated that James Spence burned trees and cleared Spence Field (another bald). It would appear that the discussion continues.

Of course, from the bald we imagined we could see Clingmans looming high above us, five miles ahead. We had a lot more work ahead of us.

From the bald we headed..DOWN...I didn't want to go down. That only meant we had to go back...UP! And up, and up to over 6600' within the next five miles! We had to go down probably 300' before we must start back up again. My mind was smoking, I was losing this head game.

Ok, it's confession time. I am lazy. Lazy and self-deluded. I have always had the belief that I could physically do just about anything I wanted. For instance, even now, at 63 years of age I figure I can do most everything I could do at 30. And at times I can. But it's kind of like the Toby Keith song, *As Good as I Once Was*. It goes something to the effect - I'm not as good as I once was, but, I'm as good once as I ever was. With a little preparation, I may be able to run a 100-yard dash, but it is highly unlikely that I could turn around and run another! I think you get the idea. Anyway, I have never been workout guy. I hate running. I hate calisthenics. I hate weight rooms. I hate gyms. Heck, I hate locker rooms. Therefore, I always default to the, I can do it without physical preparation, school of thought. Remember, I have admitted to self-delusion.

Dejectedly, I stumbled down that steep decline. Back up we trudged. I needed to stop way too often for a breath and to rest my legs. I was seriously flagged. Larry was having his own issues with painful burning in his knees. As a matter of fact, it was at this time we christened him with his designated trail name...Burning Knees.

It was at this time that Larry recalled reading backpacking sage wisdom. He had just read a book by Colin Fletcher. I believe it was *The Man Who Walked Through Time* or possibly *The Complete Walker*. Anyway, he explained, you need to become the terrain, in your mind. Don't struggle against it, become a part of it. My apologies to the late Mr. Fletcher for any injustice my paraphrasing may cause. His writings are classic.

Minds realigned, we again pressed on, now one with the trail. Passing the junction with Goshen Prong trail, we realized it was just a couple more miles to Clingmans Dome! We plodded continuing ever upward. Progress was measured, not in miles, but in yards. And it wasn't but a few hundred yards past the junction that my legs just turned to rubber, and I collapsed backward onto my pack right there in the middle of the trail.

Larry just laughed "I guess it's time for a break. Are you ok?"

"My legs just gave it up. I cannot go any farther," I puffed. "I honestly can't move. I'm done!"

Larry, "Damn, I hear someone coming down the trail"

"Screw them, I'm not moving. Hell, I'm not kidding, I can't move," I weakly laughed.

By now you probably have figured I'm full of BS. I can understand that. The next few sentences just might cement my handprints in the BS walk of fame! Bear with me on this.

Once again, I ask you to close your eyes. Now, envision this... I lay in a grassy opening, sideways across the famous Appalachian Trail. Larry, pack removed, leans against his load a few feet to the side of the trail. Around a bend in the trail, step four rugged, young, male day hikers. They walked up to my trail blocking, prone body.

"Gooday. You ok mate?" the lead hiker inquired in a thick Aussie accent.

"Sure, just taking a break," I answered. "I take it you guys aren't from around here," I astutely added.

By this time there were around seven of them gathered in front of us.

"Not at all, mate. We are with the Australian Royal Navy. We put in at Wilmington and wanted to see your Great Smoky Mountains for ourselves."

Now how cool and unexpected was that! We welcomed them to the U.S. and the Smokies, chatted briefly and they, now 15 of them, stepped over my legs, bidding us hooroo before disappearing down the trail.

Now you can open your eyes. No kidding...true story.

After a lengthy rest, I was able to regain the use of my legs and we moved on, struggling toward the peak. We made it, Clingmans Dome! Dropping our packs at the base of the observation tower, we light- heartedly walked to the observation deck. The sky was clear, and the views were unobstructed. Fontana lake was visibly winding through the valleys around ten miles to the south. Ridge after ridge, peak after peak, miles of beautiful mountain views. Wow, this alone was worth the climb. This diversion was awesome, but we had a couple more miles before we would reach Mount Collins shelter, our intended home for the night. We were feeling good, earlier trials and tribulations forgotten. However, it was already late afternoon and we needed to get moving.

The restrooms and clean water were 1/2 mile down the steep paved walking path Bob and I had traversed two years earlier. Distrust of our fellow man dictated that we hoisted our packs for the one mile round trip. We practically skipped down the trail to our destination. Refreshed and with full water supplies, we head back up the steep walkway.

It was at this point that we both came to an important realization. What a difference your mindset can make. We had just completed an excruciating, grueling 12-mile ordeal. And yet, under full pack weight, we easily traversed this climb. We couldn't help but notice that most of the unburdened day trippers, walking from the parking area were huffing, puffing, and stopping at benches to rest on their way up. Conversely, having made it to our most difficult goal, completely erased the earlier reality of being completely blown. We now glided effortlessly, under full load, back to the peak. That's the difference mindset can make.

A young couple stopped us to inquire if it was our intention to head into the backcountry? We of course answered in the affirmative.

"Have you not listened to the weather on your radio?" they asked.

"We have no radio," I answered.

"You may want to rethink your plan. There is a really bad storm coming...soon."

We thanked them for the information and their concern, assuring them of our woodsy preparedness. We started down the AT toward Mt. Collins, masking our new found sense of urgency.

Less than a mile off the summit, daylight was rapidly dimming and the wind was picking up. The conditions made the decision for us. A suitable camp site had to be established in a hurry. Weather continued to deteriorate at a rapid pace. We descended Mt. Love. The terrain was steep and level spots were nowhere to be found. A small clearing on the north side of the trail, just large enough to hold our tent would have to do. We hurriedly pitched camp with hopes of lighting the stove, using the tent for a wind break. A warm meal would do much to replenish these two wasted hikers. The rains came with a vengeance, granola bars, nuts and water it was.

Our little tent was seriously tested that night. It is hard to explain that wind. The blow was coming out of the southeast. Unfortunately, there was a draw leading from the southeast right to our tiny clearing. We missed that small detail in our haste to set camp. We could hear the wind gathering down the draw, building into what sounded like a giant wind ball rolling up the slope - bam! That ball would slam into our tent, which would shudder violently, the fiberglass supports bending until the south side of the tent would actually flatten, slapping us in our faces. Don't get me wrong, we were thankful for our nylon refuge, but at the same time, we expected our shelter to either tear into shreds at any minute, leaving us helplessly exposed to the onslaught, or to become a giant kite, flying us off of the mountain to our premature deaths. This storm was vicious and brutal. Constant lightning would light our tent as if daylight had suddenly arrived, only to be followed by total darkness and deafening, ground shaking thunder. The sound of crashing trees and limbs were a regular accompaniment. As luck would have it, we were surrounded by a tangle of scrub and small trees, no widow makers to crush our camp. An hour of unrelenting assault finally subsided into a few more hours of normal thunderstorm, complete with torrential rains.

We awoke....yes we did fall off to sleep sometime during the early morning hours, despite the bed of roots on which we had pitched the tent. A small puddle of water gathered at our feet along the downhill wall of our tent, giving the only hint of the night's tempest. Somewhat surprised, we found the tent showed no other ill effects.

Stepping out of the tent, we were greeted to a wet, misty, morning, barely illuminated by the hint of first light. Larry lit the Svea and we prepared breakfast. Warm oatmeal and hot coffee never tasted better.

I will now briefly address an incident of note, probably to no one but myself. Wanting to have a fresh start, on this fine morning, I entered our small tent to change into clean, dry clothes. Now, putting on a pair of pants while sitting down, is a process of its own. As I prepared to pull them up over my ass, I sitting/hopped up, pulled the pants to my waist and immediately returned to the ground. Excruciating pain gripped me as I had landed my full weight on a very sharp knobby root, exactly where the sun don't shine. It's kind of hard to describe the particular pain I felt at that moment. I'll only say it was not good at all. Of course, Larry just couldn't understand how that root got past my head...no respect. Those few seconds of inattention were cause for much discomfort the rest of this trip, not to mention surgery shortly after our return home, and unwanted repercussions experienced to this day. Disclaimer: Don't try this at home or on the trail.

We both felt good to go. Well, I felt good enough to get under way. Our legs felt pretty good, considering yesterday's struggles. Other than sore feet, we were ready to roll. Even our previously aching hips accepted pack weight without much complaint. That was a welcome relief. We forged on down the mysterious misty trail. Trees, large rocks, ferns and other vegetation appeared out of the white mist lending an almost prehistoric aura to our early morning expedition. Storm forgotten, we strolled through time with a renewed sense of wonder. It was an impressive morning.

Two and a half miles brought us to the junction with our next avenue of travel. We veered onto Sugarland Mountain Trail and said farewell to the fabled Appalachian Trail. It was still early morning when we reached Mt. Collins shelter 1/2- mile later. It was time for a break. We agreed, beating last night's storm to the shelter would have put us in a much better position to weather the blast. Oh well, water under the bridge.

Sugarland Mountain Trail afforded us the exact reason we decided to backpack in the first place. Narrow ridges dropping off sharply on each side, presented breathtaking views. At places, we could look back to where we had hiked, several miles earlier. Those views were truly memorable. There is nothing like actually seeing where your own feet carried you over beautifully rugged ridges and peaks, covering those miles now visibly behind you, unforgettable. For the most part the trail pleasantly descended, eventually entering hardwood forest. The day was now warm and sunny, a perfect November day. The smell of fallen leaves filled the air and the leaves themselves filled the trail. At times the leaves were knee deep, making the trail difficult to traverse. Rocks, ruts, and roots all became hidden tripping hazards. Even so, this is one of the most enjoyable trail days I can recall.

Reaching the junction with Rough Creek Trail, we left Sugarland to descend another four miles to Little River Trail, and camp site #24 (Rough Creek). Arriving at the site, we dropped our packs for a well-deserved rest. Seeing and hearing clean running mountain streams was a pleasant change from the last couple camps, and the sounds of both creeks offered natural background music. We did take advantage of the ready water source, using our new filter to replenish our supply with fresh, cold stream water. This was a large heavily used site, cleared for up to fifteen people. Being November, we had no human company that night - always a welcome situation. We laid our bedrolls out, one on each side of a small fire ring. We had supper and coffee to the added musical accompaniment of the sputtering Svea. After we cleaned up our "kitchen" and hung our food, two candle lanterns illuminated our small circle of a camp. Reclining on our bags we laughed as we relived the last few days.

Larry suddenly fell silent. He raised slightly on his elbows before quietly warning, "Don't move. There is a skunk walking up to the right of your head. I mean very close to your head."

I froze in place, while rolling my eyes to the right, cautious to not move my head. He, or she, I'll make it a she, was within inches and I could feel little skunk breaths as she sniffed my ear. I was convinced the furry little menace was going to jump on my neck and inflict a rabid attack on my jugular. Remaining stonily still, showing great courage, (read as: FROZEN WITH FEAR), I waited for her next move. Thank God... that cute critter took its last sniff, turned and walked a few feet to the fire ring. We decided to wait it out, not wanting to alarm it into a spraying defense. Our strategy worked, as nothing of interest was found in the fire pit, it simply exited stage right and down the trail. I had been practically kissed by a wild skunk and was no worse for the experience! We both had a relieved laugh, emergency averted.

That was one great night, sleeping under the stars to the flowing waters' symphony. A very pleasant four mile hike out via Little River and Cucumber Gap Trails, returned us to the Jakes Creek trailhead and the Mustang. Our 33-mile bonding relationship with Clingmans dome was complete. Both of us were one with the mountain. We shook hands in the mutual knowledge of our feat. We were backpackers!

We procured an inexpensive hotel room in Pigeon Forge...no drive thru office this time. Warm showers and clean clothes reenergized our spirits. We were ready to eat. A nearby restaurant with an all-u-can eat buffet sounded sufficient. Beef stew, fried chicken, mashed potatoes, clam chowder, chicken livers, roast beef, I'm sure you get the idea. We had set a dangerous precedent. Off the trail and into a hotel, good food and a few beers, became an enjoyable post-trail tradition.

With only a few hitches, the whole trip evolved as planned. Our new gear did the job. Man, we were feeling good about it. Ideas for the next trip were kicked around on the drive home. Now, we had both fallen in love with the Smokies and late season backpacking. Good weather (forget that silly freak storm), cooler temperatures, fewer people, more open views, virtually no bugs... perfect. And still over 800 miles of trails for us to travel.

We learned a few things that trip. We really meshed as a hiking team without even thinking about it. A well thought out circuit was quite doable. Water sources, in conjunction with our filter, could reduce the need to carry all of our water, thus reducing weight. Anything over seven miles in a day was pushing our physical limits. Australia has a Royal Navy. A small radio for weather reports was a valid piece of equipment. S**t happens. Mental discipline is a key trail companion. Skunks can whisper sweet nothings in your ear without negative effects. A sixty pound load is too heavy! Backpacking is Awesome!

Chapter 4

Close Encounter - Up in Flames

We were tweaking our gear, paring every ounce we could. Our plan would take us down as far as Fontana Lake on the North Carolina side. With good waters to fish, including some prime trout streams which emptied into the lake. Why not try the fishing thing again? Larry made aluminum rod holder tubes which we could lash to our pack frames. Collapsible rods, light spinning reels and compact tackle holders completed our angling equipment.

If we started on Clingmans Dome, our first day would be easy street...all downhill! Figuring we would be awake all day, then driving all night, then hiking the next day, downhill sounded like the perfect plan. This concept came with pouring over maps and the trail guide for the previous ten months. In all honesty, it started while driving home from the last trip.

I'm not quite sure just how to tell you about our final planning summit. First, let me explain, I am obsessed with gazing at the stars.

One night in 1973 really opened my eyes to the night sky and its possible spectacles. That late October, Friday night, I pulled into our driveway. It was 2:30 in the morning, ya, I had been hanging at my girlfriend's house a little later than I should have - don't tell my mom. Anyway, I was somewhat surprised to find my brother, Bob, laying on the hood of his 1964 Mustang, watching a meteor shower in progress. I joined him and we saw hundreds over the next hour or so. Sometimes up to 5 or more visible at the same time. What a show, it was amazing! I've seen nothing quite like it since. Thus, I remain ever vigilant.

Well, back to the evening at hand. I did allude to this in the first chapter, now, I'll just spit this out. Well, here it goes. It was midweek, late October, 1990. Sunday night was to be our scheduled launch, and we wanted to solidify departure plans. At around 10:30pm we stepped outside to let Larry's dog out. Standing in his back yard we could see our breath due to the cold temperature. The night sky was bright, and the stars were sharply visible. Perfect mood setting atmosphere for discussing our upcoming excursion.

I pointed out the lights of a Life Flight helicopter over the hospital about 1/2 mile to the southeast, as we discussed the prospect of camping under such skies in the Smokies. We conversed quietly.

"That's not a Life Flight," I noticed as the light headed in our direction. "It can't be a helicopter, there's no sound."

"You're right, what is that?"

We were in no way ready for the events of the next few minutes.

"Damn.......what the hell is that?" I said.

Larry had no answer.

This huge, triangular, wedge-shaped object was coming directly toward us! When I say huge, I mean really... really huge. As it approached, at an altitude we estimated to be no more than around 800', an extremely bright, white light illuminated the leading edge. We could actually see inside of this thing. The cockpit, I'll call it for lack of a better term, was lit up like a hospital operating room! No personnel were visible, just a brilliantly lit interior.

About that time, I'm thinking of the supposedly true story - *Fire in the Sky* - where this logger is beamed up into a UFO, right in front of his fellow loggers, only to be found dazed and naked several days later. I really didn't want to be examined and probed by some little, large eyed, gray guy with an inquisitive mind. And I was much too modest to be found naked on the street five days later. That story is scary as hell.

Anyway, what we saw was absolutely enormous, and it was no airplane or helicopter! There were single lights on the underside each of the 3 points of the wedge. It passed directly over us at a very slow speed. No sound at all...I mean complete silence. This thing was bigger than a football field, yet moving so slow, it should have fallen out of the sky. How was it staying in the air? Then we noticed something really astounding (as though what I've just told you wasn't). This is going to sound weird but, you really could not see the exterior surfaces of the object. You could see the lights, however, the object itself was only visible due to the fact that it blocked the appearance of the stars! I'm talking cloaking device invisible! The totally clear, star filled sky was perfect for revealing the shape and size of the object. It silently glided directly over us and continued on in a westerly direction and out of sight. Being the days before everyone had cell phone cameras, we could only stand there, mouths hanging open, taking it all in.

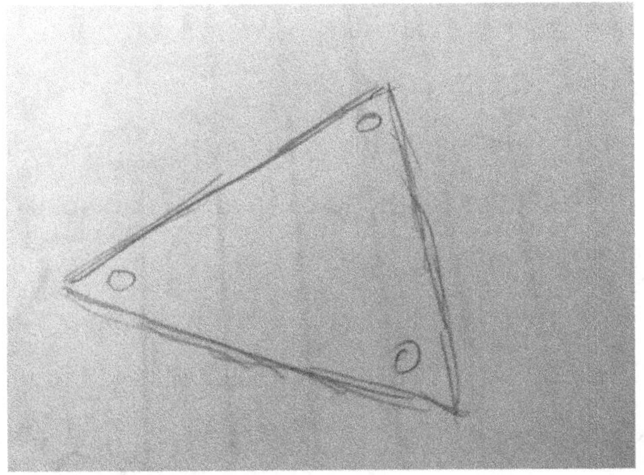

It looked something like this

I'm not sure what we saw that night. If we hadn't been planning for our next trip to the Smokies, we would have never seen that thing. It was truly one of those jaw dropping events we were lucky enough to experience. Can't explain it, just glad we saw it!

Again...True story. Ya, I know, handprints in the walk of fame. I can't really blame you. But, keep looking up... you never know.

October 29, 1990 - The Mustang was pointed south down I75 once again, we were ready to go and feeling our oats. With the same start time as last year, 6AM was our expected arrival. We had lengthy discussions about everything from the Cleveland Browns and Indians, our just finished, youth football season, work, family, the upcoming trek and of course our mysterious back yard encounter, over coffee and sandwiches. Easy and uneventful, the trip was a breeze.

We made our Sugarland Welcome Center stop, and started the winding 40 minute trip up to Clingmans Dome. We were parked at the trailhead by 7:30am. We unloaded our gear and prepared for the trail. It was shaping up to be a wonderful fall day! Dawn was crisp and cold. Fog blanketed the valleys below. The aroma of fresh mountain air, fir trees, and fallen leaves dropped by thousands, heck probably millions of deciduous trees, greeted our senses. It was good to be back.

With everything lashed, mounted and strapped on, we took our first steps of the day. At 10.6 miles, it was an ambitious goal. However, being all downhill, all day, this would be a stroll in the park. Nodding in readiness, we made our way onto Forney Ridge Trail. Just a little over a mile into the trip we passed the junction with Forney Creek trail and then the trail took an upward attitude. After climbing gradually over the next 3/4 mile, we leveled onto Andrews Bald. Andrews is supposed to be a picturesque grassy bald with great views of the valleys below. Unfortunately, the fog prevented our sightseeing. We spent a little time on the bald in order to readjust equipment and take a breather. Hell, I was already winded, and my shoes didn't feel quite right. But, the trail was calling. I'm not quite sure how to explain the feelings I experienced during the first few miles of a new outing. Excited, anxious, contented, apprehensive...they all applied.

It would be a steady descent from here. Pretty much dropping 500' per mile. Soon I called for a break. The angle of decent along with my 250 pounds of total weight had my feet sliding forward into the front of my lightweight hiking boots, causing pain and of course blisters. After removing socks and shoes, I readjusted everything and tightened my laces for more stability. Despite the obvious pain, on we went.

My quads and feet were screaming at me. Larry's quads were feeling it, but his knees were in real pain. We had slightly miscalculated the "downhill effect." Of course, the farther we went, the more tired, more sore, and more accident prone we became. Kicking into tree roots and rolling ankles on rocks as we encountered obstacles hidden under fallen leaves, did nothing to improve our condition.

The trail was wide enough, but it was like walking in a stream bed, filled with rocks of every shape, hidden beneath several inches of fallen leaves. Add tree roots and the steep grade along with constant sliding over rolling rocks while kicking bigger rocks and roots, and you have a recipe for great discomfort, if not disaster. A stroll in the park, it was not.

We finally made the 5.7- mile mark and the end of Forney Ridge Trail. Slouching our packs off we leaned back on a couple of trees for a well needed break.

Larry laughed, "All I hear is the thunk of your footsteps, followed by cussing at tree roots and rocks. You sound like an ill-tempered Big Foot."

"Every time I kick something, my boot smashes into my big toe. Damned excruciating." I looked at my already bleeding toenail. "If this continues, I will be in deep trouble."

Jerky and granola bars were lunch. Messing with anything more just wasn't an interesting option at the time. During our 30 minute down time, I worked to address my blisters and rubbed my aching feet with alcohol to cool and dry them. Oh ya, and remove the blood from my toes. Ah, things felt better. I was ready to get back on the trail. Although, truthfully I would have loved to be done for the day, I had to take it as it came.

We had roughly 5.5 more miles to go on Springhouse Branch Trail. Camp site #71 (CCC) 2180', would be a welcome stop. Man I hated the last few miles of that day. Who would believe it, I was wishing for just a small uphill run. But we were like horses heading to the barn, getting there as quickly as we could, stumbling, tripping, and complaining, we finally encountered the chimney remains of the old CCC camp that is site #71. Noticing a small tent barely visible off to the east, we chose our site on the western end in order to assure quiet and solitude. With sighs of relief, we dropped our packs, elated to be off our feet, done for the day! We had actually made good time. We still had a couple hours of daylight to set up camp and cook supper.

We stripped off our boots and socks for a quick cool-down before heading back to our water source for the night. My socks were a sweat and blood-soaked mess. Damn my feet were soft. The constant shifting and rubbing in my shoes had removed way too much skin from the tops and sides of my toes and the backs of my heels. And my nails on my big toes, especially my right, had been jammed back into my toes. It felt like both had been smashed by hammer blows! The right nail was already turning black. Neither of us thought this to be a good thing. I carried that black nail on my right foot for the next year and a half. Badge of honor...or stupidity, you be the judge.

At times like these we were glad that we both elected to carry a light weight pair of "camp" shoes. What a welcome relief to have light, flexible, dry shoes for the evening chores. We backtracked (limped) a short distance to the water source to refill our bottles, our pot for the evening meal and coffee, and wash our overly abused socks. Cold fresh water is a wonderful thing. We filtered our drinking water then filled our cooking pots and returned to camp.

Being that this site used to be an old CCC (Civilian Conservation Corps) camp back in the 1930s, it did have some interesting leftover artifacts. An old chimney and fireplace still stood. A bathtub and old foundation stones, along with an old dump still remained. Of course, the ever present modern trash was also present. Overall it was an interesting piece of the past.

Firewood was gathered, the tent erected, and our sleeping gear arranged to air-out and "loft" while we ate. A fire was lit mainly to dry our socks and shoes. We typically avoided campfires, preferring to evade the inherent hazards, while gaining extended night vision, and better star gazing. Larry arranged a drying rack of sticks and hung our socks to dry by the fire. His boots were absolutely soaked from a soggy stream crossing, so he leaned them carefully on a rock allowing for maximum drying.

That night we did cook over the fire. Cooking consisted of heating water to add to our dehydrated beef stew. Leaning back against our packs, we found that a stout limb could be jammed into the ground and the other end braced against the pack frame made for a comfortable recliner with the addition of a RidgeRest pad for a seat, we enjoyed that stew. It seemed like the best meal ever!

Leaning back and enjoying a cup of after dinner coffee, we were reminiscing on the day's events. We were kings of the trail...We had it all!

Suddenly surprised by a person addressing us from our right.........

"Hello in camp."

There stood an older woman holding a pot in her hand. Well, older than I was at the time.

Being good trail emissaries, we met her smiling face with our own hospitable greeting. "Welcome to our camp. How are you doing this fine evening?"

She nonchalantly pointed to our blaze ....."Your socks are on fire," She politely informed us.

"Oh damn it!" Larry jumped up to remove the blazing socks. Equally embarrassing was the fact that his shoes were smoking and starting to melt!

We all had a good laugh at our rather unsavvy camp misfortune. While parts of Larry's shoes were a bit deformed, we assessed they would still be trail worthy. And we did still have two half pairs of socks.

"Since your dinner has burned," she quipped with a smile. "My husband and I would like to offer some leftover rice and hot peppers."

We couldn't refuse such an offer from a wonderfully smart assed, fellow camper. Our kind of people! Filling our bowls with the savory medley, we tasted the rice, and both found it to be quite hot and extremely tasty. Giving her our culinary thumbs up, we thanked both her and her absent husband for their kind offering, shared another laugh, and bid a fond good evening.

We finished the rice with great reverence for their camp fare talents! We rehashed the day's trials, mishaps, and triumphs over a second cup of coffee. Darkness had set in and stars were revealing themselves through the bare limbs of surrounding forest. It was another beautiful night in the

Smokies. Man, the trail just has a way of opening your mind to the beauties of nature and good hard physical efforts. Despite one pair of slightly deformed shoes and the loss of two pairs of socks, it was a really good start to the trip. Battered feet and all, we hit the beds that night with a smile, content in the knowledge that we were in new territory, and had survived another 10 plus mile day. That was a satisfying tired.

Daylight broke dimly, illuminating a dense fog. Our breakfast water heated over the sputtering Svea. As usual, our morning fuel consisted of Coffee and oatmeal. Quickly and quietly we broke camp, not wanting to disturb our fellow campers. We refilled our water bottles and hiked south on Forney Creek Trail. The morning was pleasant and quiet. Only the sound of the flowing creek and our footfalls broke the foggy silence. The plan was to travel about a mile on Forney Creek Trail before peeling off on White Oak Branch Trail for approximately 2 miles. Then take the Lakeshore Trail west for 1.25 miles where our camp on Fontana Lake, #74 awaited our arrival. A day under 5 miles sounded pretty good.

The morning wore on. Humid heat quickly replaced the cool of the morning as the fog burned off. Somehow we got confused as on what was to be a short, direct trail. I have a way of making that happen. Unsure that we were even on the correct trail at that point (blazes were not evident), we noticed a fairly worn trail heading up a grade to our right. Seeming like a good choice, we took a chance. The trail quickly opened to a hillside clearing. We had inadvertently stumbled onto a large area of bare dirt which we originally thought to be cleared and plowed to be farmed. However, it soon became evident that it was a cemetery, probably from early 1900's and possibly mid to late 1800's. Many of the stones were just that, small and weathered with no visible markings. Realizing we were on hallowed ground we paused to reflect on the lives of the people that had settled and died here. We could only imagine how difficult their lives must have been in this remote mountainous area. Of course, the nearby lake would not have existed yet, and logging would have been the main industry in the latter years before the National Park was established. In fact, many of the trails in this part of the mountains were either logging roads or rail beds built probably by the CCC in those years. We departed, thankful that our poor navigational skills had led us there. Poor navigational skills seem to be a constant reoccurring subject.

Earlier in the Spring of that year we meticulously planned a trip to the Daniel Boone National Forest in Kentucky. Ordering topo and trail maps, we decided to backpack and fish a section of the Sheltowee Trace. From the start of this trek we were slightly unsure of the trail. That particular section was poorly marked to completely unmarked. We "bushwhacked" our way along the steam, tossing a few lures to no effect. It was hot, humid and buggy. The trail was in a very narrow valley, steeply rising on both sides. Within about 6 miles we had to cross the stream 8 times or more. It was slow going and not the enjoyable hike we had planned. As the day wound down the trail entered an open, wide pasture-like valley with the stream winding to the east side, against a rather large cliff around 50 feet in height. We pitched camp on the western edge of the valley with a picturesque view of the broad grassy flats and the cliff. Feeling much better about the day, we watched the bright, full moon reveal itself over the ridge. Such views tend to make rough days worth the effort. The night was turning cold as we zipped in. We were suddenly awakened by several laughing voices. Most of the voices passed our position, however, two paused nearby and their conversation mentioned our tent. Knives drawn, we went on high alert as they wondered aloud as to if anyone might be inside. All right...we do have trust issues. Quietly we unzipped our tent. There sat two male hikers catching their breath and talking as others continued by, full size ice chests, boom boxes, guitars, lawn chairs, and other various items of comfort, in hand. There had to be at least seven or more of them. Not at all what we expected in this remote location! They all continued up the valley loudly talking, singing and laughing. For several hours we were serenaded with shouts, hoots, laughing and music from their stereo. Ah, nature at its finest. Waking to a frozen morning valley, we quickly packed up to remove ourselves far from our fellow campers. Rounding a bend in the trail we were astonished to find we had camped within a couple hundred yards of a back road. How did we miss that small detail? Oh ya...POOR NAVIGATIONAL SKILLS!

Back in the Smokies, considering the cemetery was not a marked feature on our trail map, we were still rather confused as to our location. Descending the cemetery access trail, we rejoined the trail from which we first arrived, whatever that was. The trail was trending south and thus toward the lake. Thus we felt we were on the correct trail. Then path looped east and became thin and appeared to be less traveled. Hot, sweaty, and somewhat troubled by our unknown position, we chose to take a break, refuel, and assess our next move. I opened an apple granola bar and my water bottle for my midmorning snack. Discussing the trails while looking at the map, we were alerted by the sound of something crashing through the brush. Suddenly a young deer ran to within 10 feet of us and stopped, just staring at us. I slowly extended my snack as an offering, guessing that the scent of apple from my granola had initiated this encounter. After raising its nose slightly and sniffing a few times, our visitor decided to turn and quickly vacated our resting spot. Our spirits suddenly seemed lighter, due to the surprise encounter. Laughing, we folded our map, secure that our decision to continue on our current trail would bring us to a junction with the main trail. Well, as secure as we usually are considering our lack of directional intuition.

Miraculously our decision panned out and we soon encountered a sign pointing us toward site #74 (Lower Forney 1720'). The sound and sight of a large rushing mountain stream gave great promise as to our home for the night. Within a quarter of a mile the trail opened with a view of our site. Wow... a thunderous stream, more like a river, widened to around twenty feet or more rushing around huge boulders for approximately 100 yards before emptying into Fontana Lake.

Fontana Lake had been drained down for the winter just as I found with Douglas Lake three years earlier. Thus, many feet of lakebed was available for exploration. We were on the west side of a "finger cove" almost a mile from the main lake body. The exposed bed on both sides of the cove were very steep, but the west side was somewhat terraced due to many levels of the drain-down. The east side was pretty much straight up into immediate forest. Mountains rose on three sides of camp, while the lake bordered on the east. Due to the fact that in season boaters use this site, there were a couple of picnic tables available, along with large fire rings.

We were in heaven as we pitched camp and cooled our tired aching feet in that magnificent stream. The sounds of crashing water would be our serenade for the night! I have since camped at many amazing places...Toroweap overlook on the North Rim of the Grand Canyon, The Badlands in

South Dakota, the Little Florida mountains in New Mexico, Beaverhead

mountains in Montana... and I still consider #74 to be one of my favorites.

We found numerous deer and bear tracks while exploring the exposed lakebed. The promise of visiting bears was an exciting possibility. A dry lakebed revealed many interesting, once hidden, secrets. One such secret being a look at bottom structure hidden in the depths during the summer months. Deep channels, stumps, rocks ridges and depressions were exposed. I also found nice mineral specimens such as kyanite, petrified wood, and quartz. Being within the boundaries of the National Park, collecting such items would be illegal. I am an avid rock hound, and leaving such items behind was disappointing, but restraint was practiced! Being a dammed and flooded valley, remnants of old settlements, towns and homesteads are possible finds. I have even heard of past American Indian sites being found including flint tools and arrowheads on exposed lakebed. Now that would be exciting! We headed back to camp, hot and tired, after an afternoon of exploration. Fishing became an afterthought.

That was a darn near perfect night. Laying there with a cup of coffee, star gazing, the occasional shooting star, and the roaring of the river, that was a very memorable camp.

The next day would take us 1300' up the mountain in about 5.5 miles. Other than the typical late October early morning fog along the lake, fairly nice, although cool weather was the order of the day. However, Forney Creek was running heavy due to rains at higher elevations.

One creek crossing gave us cause for concern. The stream was wide and deep, with no desirable options for a crossing. We had to rock hop on the small exposed tops of three questionably spread boulders. After contemplating the removal clothes, and attempting to wade the deep, swift flow, we deemed it too risky and elected the hop.

Larry, the first to attempt the crossing, made the precarious jump to the first boulder and wobbled to a steady base, prior to contemplating the second leap. He voiced some doubt about the length of the next jump. After deciding retreat was not an option, he gathered himself, and pushed off...

"S**t!" - echoed throughout the immediate forest as he clung to the top of the second rock, the lower half of his body submerged in the swiftly flowing waters.

I was not exactly sure what my course of action should be. His heavy pack was not really helping matters, I was amazed as he pulled himself onto the rock and composed himself for the final leap.

"Damn that's cold."

"Well, be careful of your footing. You sure you can make it?"

"Too late to second guess now. Here it goes."

He hit the last rock and continued, jumping safely onto the other bank. We both laughed as I looked around, rethinking my options. Larry expressed doubts as to the viability of completing the second jump, and I was giving that serious consideration. My concern was greatly heightened, considering, the longest jump now had a wet landing area. Footing would be dubious at best. Seeing no alternative, I leaped into the task at hand. After landing on the first rock, I now realized just how far the second rock was. No... no... no... I did not want to find myself dangling off that boulder, half submerged. Or worse yet, smashing my face on that rocky menace, only to live out my toothless life, ashamed of a failed pitiful effort. I gathered myself and leaped for all I had. Amazed, I found myself standing high and dry. Yes! I finished the crossing, glad to be dry and fully toothed.

Larry shiveringly expressed his surprise at my successful crossing. I too was pleasantly impressed. We now looked for a suitable area where he could change clothes and dry off. Naked and shivering, Larry searched his pack for a dry set of clothes, glad that his pack remained above the waterline throughout the ordeal. Of course, it was at that exact minute that we heard voices of nearby hikers heading our way. Why?...We hadn't seen or heard another human since the first night's flaming sock fiasco. And yet, the minute Larry took his clothes off in the middle of a trail, it was time to entertain guests! It was kind of like watching a slightly overweight, full grown man, playing naked hopscotch against a time clock.

I had a similar event a few years earlier, when Larry and I went winter fishing in a state park near our hometown. It was snow covered as we headed down a steep trail to the river. We were heading upriver toward the dam where saugeye would stack up that time of year. I had put on winter clothes, including long underwear, and I was sweating like crazy. What the heck it was early morning and we were in thick river bottom, so I decided to shed a layer. You guessed it... pants and long johns off and... voices out of nowhere, coming my way! I never got pants on so fast. Just in time as a young female park ranger leading a guided youth walk waived a friendly hello. All I

could think is pantless old guy...young kids...state park...
prison! Crisis averted. How does this happen?

Larry skillfully hopped, jumped, and scurried into those
clothes just as our fellow folks of the trail rounded the
bend. He beat the clock!

We warned them of the stream crossing ahead. They
thanked us and continued on their way. Finding a suitable
place, we stopped to allow for some drying of Larry's
clothes while we took a break.

With no further mishaps, we made it to our night's camp,
#69 (Huggins 2800'). Forney and Huggins Creeks meet
here, a nice open area with a good water source. This
would be a good quiet place for the night. We safely dried
Larry's shoes, socks and pants. Flamelessly, I might add.

We threw a few lures into some promising pools with no
luck, then settled in for an uneventful night.

The next day's hike followed an old logging road and
rail bed. It was a pleasant uphill day. We camped at #68
(Steel Trap 3960'). This is a decent site with a good water
source. It was a nice clear cool evening and star gazing
through the leafless treetops was very good that night. We
both drifted off around 10 pm. I suddenly woke, startled by
lights shining down the trail toward us.

I slapped Larry awake, "What the hell, there are headlights coming down the trail!" I pointed up the trail. "There aren't supposed to be vehicles on this trail!"

"That is bright," Larry said, also surprised by the advancing lights. He watched intently for several seconds. "You moron, that's the moon!"

It was just now clearing a ridge enough to expose it's bright, pure white rim. Laughing, we watched as the intensely bright natural light began to illuminate the entire forest. I don't believe I have ever seen the moon give off such light to this day. I guess it was what's called a super moon. We still laugh about my new phobia...oncoming moonlight.

After a leisurely breakfast we broke camp to tackle a 3500' climb over just 3 miles. That was a slow plodding day. We made it without mishap. Collapsing back in the Clingmans Dome parking lot, we shed our gear and regained some energy. Clingmans tower offered a great view of where we had stomped during the past several days.

Surveying our surroundings from that tower, we felt pretty darn good about our accomplishment. Over thirty miles, from "The Dome", down to where the rushing waters of Forney Creek empty into Fontana Lake, and back to the top. We recovered in the old CCC camp, observing relics from early logging efforts. Treasures of the dry lakebed revealed themselves to us. Fabulous night skies entertained and amazed us. We survived a perilous stream crossing, with no injury, and Larry winning the race of saved modesty. We saw where early settlers of the area both lived and where they rest in death. We dodged the onrushing full moon. We roasted socks and shoes. How many people can live all of that in a few days? It was another great trip!

Chapter 5

High Times, High Winds, and
Hypothermia-
Dance of the Marionette

The call of the Great Smokies beckoned us again. Four years had passed since the "burning sock incident." Fall and winter backpack hunting trips in a section of National Forest in southern Ohio had consumed our available time. Primitive winter camping and hunting in and around a rock overhang with a 100-acre lake within a few hundred feet was hard to resist. Being just four hours from home made short two to four-day trips close at hand. But those trips are stories for another time. Even as we spent a late Autumn weekend squirrel hunting in that southern Ohio refuge, Larry and I, flintlocks resting across our laps, discussed how the sight and smell of the falling leaves and warmth of the October sun made us both long for a return trip to The Smokies. The gears were set in motion.

We gathered our equipment and prepared for a 3-day trip in the northeast section of the park. Larry mapped out a route starting in the Cosby Camp area. Following Gabes Mountain Trail, we would experience old growth forest. Maddron Bald trail would offer more of the same while bringing us to Snake Den Ridge. Who could resist an area with a name like that? All told, less than 20 miles in three days. We were both excited at the prospects of an all new area and our first December trip in the Smokies.

Gripped in anticipation, we once again headed down I71. This time we were in my 1985 3/4- ton Chevy conversion van. There was plenty of room for gear, and it could serve as sleeping quarters if the need arose.

We rolled through Cincinnati laughing as we recalled our earlier trip to Kentucky.

I had gotten very serious about paring weight from my pack. I went through every item in my kit and decided to discard anything I hadn't used on previous excursions. Even items as small as extra keys were left behind. Only first aide items were exempt. Water and food included, my pack weight was down to a respectable 40 pounds. Beat the heck out of the usual 60 pounds I had been carrying. We were still traveling in my old Mustang at that time. Passing through Cincinnati at 2am, I pulled off for a fuel stop. I jumped out, grabbed the pump handle, and opened the fuel filler door...Damn...the locking gas cap. I forgot about the locking gas cap! One of the keys I removed during my weight cutting mania? I kept going over each of the 2 keys left on my key ring. Mustang...house...Mustang...house. No matter how many times I looked and wished, that little silver key just wasn't there. I couldn't have done that. How ridiculous. Reality set in.

Larry looked at me in disbelief, "Really, you took that key off to save weight? You are kidding right? You can't be that stupid!" He reluctantly laughed.

"Oh, yes...yes I can."

We spent the next 30 minutes with screw drivers and vice grips in hand, trying to remove that very secure cap, expecting Cincinnati's finest to stop by at any time. Of course, the thought of a spark from our prying efforts, was cause for apprehension in us both. I kept thinking how well this locking cap worked. Finally successful, we now had another problem. The cap was ruined in our attempt to gain entry. I went in the station and ask the attendant if they sold gas caps. No deal, but she did have a box of caps others had left behind. Damn, they were all radiator caps. Really, nobody left a gas cap behind? Unbelievably, one not only fit, but worked for the rest of the time I owned that Mustang! Ah, good times.

Back to the trip at hand. We arrived at Cosby early in the morning as usual. We were very excited to be back in The Smokies after our four year hiatus. Man, it was good to be there. Cosby is a "bowl" at around 2000' of elevation, surrounded by mountains as high as 5500'. What a beautiful sight. Such places always fill me with a sense of wonder and a need to find out what I can find around the next bend and over the next rise. Just knowing we were on our way up there was cause for great anticipation. We hoped to be up to the challenge. The first day would be around 4.8 miles with a 1200' climb in elevation. We could handle that.

Temperatures were quite warm for December. Blue and sunny skies welcomed us as we stepped onto the trail. The miles passed reluctantly. We were both rather tired after eight hours on the road. That particular night trip seemed to take it out of me for sure. Later in the day's hike we started seeing some older growth forest. Those enormous old hemlock trees lend to an almost mystical aura. Our steps and loads lightened due to our heightened interest in the spectacle of these majestic trees. We entered site #34 (Sugar Cove) exhilarated by both the beauty of the last few miles and the fact that we were done for the day. The site was fairly flat and welcoming with a nice stream for cleanup, cool down, and clean cold drinking water. Once again, being late in the year, it appeared we would camp alone. We both considered that to be ideal.

We hung our food bag as usual. Each of us found a nub of a branch to hang our packs on smaller trees in camp. It was a cool clear evening. We pitched our tent but decided to sleep under the stars with the tent as a backup plan in case of rain. I had forgotten just how magical these mountains were. Coyotes howled in the distance as a mouse scurried around camp keeping us company. Hands behind my head, I laid there watching stars showing through tangled limbs, very tired, but relaxed and content.

We woke to an overcast forty- degree morning, glad we had dodged the rain. The forecast, however, was calling for it all day. I pulled my pack from its tree bound hanger. Damn...our friendly little campmate chewed a hole through the storm flap! My beloved Camp Trails pack had been defiled. How could he be so thoughtless? And we had treated him as a welcome friend. At least he found nothing of any use to him and had left all else unscathed. Larry got a kick from my anti-mouse tirade. I was a bit overzealous as I recall.

Of course, it is a well- known fact that a hammer and duct tape can fix just about anything. Not having a hammer, I pulled some duct tape from our "emergency repair kit" and Shazam... just like new! The color was almost a perfect match and the waterproof integrity of my pack was once again intact. Feeling much better, breakfast was prepared, and our day was properly underway. The trail out of camp was a steady descent of around 500' in 5 miles. There we joined the Maddron Bald Trail. By this time, it was raining heavily and the temperature remained just under 50 degrees. We broke out the rain suits, pack covers, and continued on. The first couple miles of this trail was actually gravel roadbed. I would like to tell you this made for easy travels, but the grade was a steady climb and the added sweating brought on by the rain gear worked against me.

I have never liked wearing rain protection. I tend to run on the warm side and am uncomfortable with added layers. I have hiked in very cold weather. While others wore coats, stocking hats, long johns and gloves, I have hiked in a t-shirt covered by a light-weight nylon shirt with the sleeves rolled up, light weight pants and a light hat. I cannot wear gloves or insulated gear as I overheat quickly. I sweat so much in "breathable" rain gear that I become as wet as if I didn't wear it at all.

Within around 2 miles of this trail, we came to the junction with Albright Grove Loop Trail. This 0.7- mile loop trail follows through some huge virgin forest. While our original intent was to take in the loop, the weather led us to put the added mileage on the back burner, fodder for a future trip.

The rain was now pouring relentlessly. The trail became a creek of its own as we climbed higher. We continued, wading, splashing and rock hopping over deeper puddles. The wind kicked up, howling out of the south, driving the rain at us face on. While I do like a challenge, these conditions were wearing on me. I believe Larry concurred. Roughly 7 miles into the days trial, we entered campsite #29 (Otter Creek4960').

At this point we considered pulling up short, and laying down camp there. However, we found this site to be steep, muddy, wet, and overall uninviting. Giving up on this as our overnight accommodations, we still decided it was necessary to throw up a tarp lean-to. We needed to block the wind and rain, replenish energies, and warm ourselves. Drying out did not seem to be a viable option.

We were able to find a somewhat level spot with usable limbs for erecting a three-sided shelter which actually blocked most of the elements. Soaked, cold, and tired, Larry lit the Svea and prepared a pot of minestrone soup. That soup felt like life saving nectar going down. The needed warmth greatly improved our standing both physically, and mentally. It became obvious that wishing the rain and wind away would not make it so. Larry made another pot of soup probably as a subconscious tactic, delaying our departure. We devoured the second with as much relish as the first. Revisiting the conversation on putting up camp for the night, we again decided to push on. Snake Den Ridge was about 1.5 miles further up the trail, and 800' - 1000' gain in elevation.

Tentatively, we dismantled our makeshift shelter, packed up, and trudged away from our "soup oasis". Fearing hypothermia, I continued to wear my woefully inadequate rain gear in an effort to conserve body heat. It didn't seem to have any ability to shed water, but did keep me in a state of overheat. Larry had heavier rainwear which performed its job better than mine. As an added plus, he doesn't suffer from the same body temp malady as I. The climb was torturous in those conditions. I was constantly pausing to catch my breath and cool down.

From several yards in front of me, Larry hailed through the wind that we were about to enter Maddron Bald. We were now taking the wind, which was screaming up out of the valley on our right, at full force as we stepped onto the bald, protected only be waist high myrtle bushes. Winds assaulted us face-on at what we estimated to be 30 plus mph. And with the temperature now at 45, we had a wind chill of 35 or less. Wow, that bald was brutal. Our soaked bodies were quickly feeling the effects. We had to yell over the wind and our loudly flapping rain suits in order to communicate. We figured that our intended destination could be within a mile.

My movements were becoming increasingly sluggish and labored. I was falling back even further than usual. While it was not unusual for my pace to be slower than just about anyone I've hiked with, I was now moving, truly at a snail's pace. I was feeling lethargic and just plain tired. The wind, rain, and cold were unrelenting. As the day wore on, Larry pressed forward, eager to find our stop for the night. After what seemed like hours, I saw him in a small grassy clearing, pack dropped against a tree. Thank God... that must be the place. A few moments later, I collapsed against that same tree and unstrapped my pack.

"We need to throw up the tent and a wind break," Larry hollered through the wind..

I continued to sit, unmoved by his urging.

Pulling essential items from his pack, "Come on...we need to get this thing up!" He now barked with annoyance.

"Ya, ya," I answered as I slowly pulled myself up and worked at removing the tent from my pack. Tent removed from its restraints, I sat back against the tree.

Larry worked quickly at erecting a tarp wind break. "What are you doing? Get over here and help me put this thing up!" He yelled.

I faintly remember the tarp being ripped from our hands more than once by blasting gusts. We gave up on the wind break and I sat back against the tree. I was fuzzy headed, and quite frankly, I remember being content to sit there and rest.

Next it was time for the tent! My hands would not cooperate with the task at hand. On top of that, I could not focus my thoughts at all. I fumbled with the chore at hand until Larry told me to just sit back down while he got the tent set up. I really didn't care if that damn tent got set up or not. I just wanted to lay down and go to sleep. Rain, wind... it didn't matter. I just wanted to close my eyes.

I don't remember much other than Larry telling me to get out of my wet clothes and into my sleeping bag. He pretty much forced me to eat a couple granola bars and drink quite a bit of water. That was like a magic elixir. I became somewhat coherent, and felt warm and cozy, cocooned in my bag, as the unrelenting rain pelted the tent in wind driven sheets. At that point, I felt ashamed and downright gutless. I had given in to the effects of hypothermia way too easily. Hell, if it wasn't for Larry's ability to take care of the situation, in those miserably adverse conditions, I might have just given up the ghost right there on Snake Den Ridge! Well done, and thank you.

I hate to be melodramatic, but now my life may have actually been saved by each of my brothers.

When I was around 10, my mom decided I should learn to swim. My older brother, Bob, had already taken lessons and was enrolled in advanced classes. I was to be in beginners - class, but the class was already full. I was placed in the advanced class with the understanding that the instructor would work with my short comings. The very first day we were taken to the deep end where we were one by one, to jump in and swim back to the ladder on the side of the pool. How difficult could that be? When it was my turn, I gave it my best leap. I wanted to show those older guys my jumping ability. Up and out I went, then down into the beautifully clear, shimmering water. Straight to the bottom. I flailed and struggled and never got anywhere at all. Through the wavy water I could blearily make out that shining sunlit silver ladder and a few heads peering over the edge. Panic was setting in and I was about to watch all 10 years of my life flash before my eyes. Bob, in his wise brotherly insight, realized I was acting more like a brick than a swimmer. We were the only ones that seemed to grasp the concept that I was drowning! Without hesitation, he dove in and pulled me to the surface, where I gasped and chocked, very glad to be back on dry land and breathing air. I was from that time forward, relegated to a kickboard in the shallows. I did not complain.

As I write this, Bob has passed on after a battle with cancer, just a few short months ago. He is truly missed. And I may have failed to tell him thanks for his efforts that day. Big Brother, I say it now...thank you. I'll see you on the other side.

Back on Snake Den Ridge we were awakened in the middle of the night by the distinctly heaver sounds of the tent being pelted by hail. It was definitely much colder, and we were in a heavy, freezing rain. Having regained what little wits I have, we both figured this wasn't the best situation to be in. Once again, we hoped our inexpensive, two season tent could take the strain. We discussed how unexpected this weather was. I guess in hindsight we might have expected something like this could happen 5000' up on a mountain in December. Oh well, we went back to sleep, listening to the drumming of the icy rain.

The morning dawned extremely still, quiet, and dark. Larry crawled out of his sleeping bag, slipped on his boots, and unzipped the tent fly.

"You aren't going to believe this." The fly opened with a crunching sound, revealing a brilliant, white, high-country scene.

"Holy smoke! That has to be 5" of snow!"

We had no idea any snow had fallen. Hurrying to step outside we were welcomed to one of the most beautiful camp sites I have ever seen. Everything was blanketed in a full 5" of pure, beautiful, pristine, white snow. The tent looked like our own personal igloo. Bushes, trees, rocks, everything was blanketed in snow. I walked over and picked up my canteen, which I had foolishly left against a tree in my stupor the previous evening. Brushing the snow off, I found it completely encrusted in ice and the contents frozen solid. Temps had really taken a dive that night. In fact, as we prepared and ate our breakfast of coffee and oatmeal, the thermometer on my pack dropped from the warm reading of 34° within our tent to 25°. It was no wonder everything was frozen.

We had to physically beat on the tent in order to dislodge the snow and hidden layer of ice beneath. That was one very rigid tent. Everything was frozen, including our tarp/ground cloth, which actually cracked as we attempted to fold it! The shock corded poles were completely frozen together. We tried breathing on the joints in order to thaw them, to no avail. Finally, in desperation, we whacked them against a tree thinking that might vibrate them free. Nope... shattered fiberglass was the result. At least they were short enough to lash on and pack out. Being responsible backpackers, we left nothing behind, to defile our no trace campsite. Once again, that inexpensive two season tent had taken natures onslaught! We took the stout winds and substantial extra weight of the snow and ice in stride. I have to give credit where credit is due!

Temps being 25° , we both started out with gloves, stocking hats, and insulated shirts. Within 15 minutes we were in t- shirts, and the gloves and hats were removed. Larry chose to go hatless. However, my lack of hair dictates that I always wear a light hat or suffer sinus consequences. Memories of yesterday's ugly weather conditions gave way to the tranquil beauty of the snow covered mountains. Snowy, overhanging tree limbs magically transformed our trail into a white tunnel winding ever downward. Our moods were light, and we thoroughly enjoyed the morning's hike. There was one negative. Rocks, roots, and uneven areas hidden from view by the snow and the icy layer coating everything under the snow, made for tenuous footing. To make things worse, Larry had new boots with a sole billed as one of the best. They had conversely, proven to be quite unsure on wet surfaces. Truthfully, they were downright slippery.

We gingerly picked our way down the trail. Rounding a bend to the right, a view of Cosby Valley opened up below us. The vista was breathtaking. The valley floor showed some green while everything else surrounding it lay in a thick, white, blanket of snow. What a morning! We were both glad to get a chance to experience this event firsthand. Taking a break, we savored the view a bit longer, realizing what an unexpectedly special affair this trip had become. I suppose many might have considered the cold and snow to be an annoyance at best. We certainly did not.

As we descended, it was warming up. Temps had risen into the low 30s. Moving ahead, we noted the snow was thinning and in some small areas, rocks were visible. We were probably about 2000' lower than last night's 25°, snow and ice covered, post-hypothermic, oasis.

We suddenly halted. Damn, at first glance, it appeared to be the stream crossing from hell! We both realized our situation suddenly looked a bit more daunting. Not tremendously wide, and with several rocks precariously spaced for hopping, what could go wrong? Couldn't be more than twelve feet wide. There were a few complications though. A placid, but fairly deep pool was on the right. A fall there would mean complete emersion, wet gear, and another chance at hypothermia. Unfortunately, to the left an even greater danger waited, a steep drop of ten to twelve feet with large boulders and jagged rocks to break any unfortunate hiker's fall. Neither prospect looked particularly pleasing. Oh ya, and Larry's shoes could pass for ice skates on the wet rocks offered as our crossing. Also, the possibility of a skim of ice on any of the rocks was still not out of the question.

Upstream, downstream, we could find no viable alternative. We dropped our packs and sat down to contemplate any possible way to avoid the inevitable. Nervously we decided to bite the bullet and get to it. Being the sure footed "goat boy" of the two of us, I would be the first to give it a try.

We retied our boots, put our packs back on, and cinched them as tight as we could in order to alleviate as much weight shift as possible. Positioning myself in line with the rocky runway, I prepared for takeoff. The possibility of a mistake leading to a fall to the left was a bit distracting, I fully admit. With a three step start, I ran and jumped for that first rock. Land, gather, jump... land, gather, jump...land, gather, jump...land, gather, jump...land, gather, jump...land... made it! I finally breathed for the first time since that first jump. It was a sigh of relief. I would be lying if I said that an error on the side of the rock drop wasn't on my mind the whole way across.

Larry nervously laughed. "Damn you are a goat. You made that look easy!"

"It's not too bad," I answered. "Just be careful. The spacing isn't as bad as it looks. But, watch those damn shoes."

Larry gave one last tug on his pack straps, gathered, and steeled himself for his fateful attempt. I was sincerely afraid that his footing would fail on the very first rock, sending him splashing into that ice cold pool. I had dropped my pack, preparing for any needed extraction or first aid measures.

My stomach tightened as he took the first hop. One rock...two...three, I was starting to relax, his technique was flawless. Then, as his right foot hit the forth rock, his left leg kicked up and his body teetered leaning left toward the rocky drop. My mind suddenly flashed as to how I was going to drag his dead body up out of those rocks and down the trail to the parking lot. Worse yet, how was I going to explain any of this to his wife and kids! Oh yes, those really were my exact thoughts at that moment.

Suddenly his body pivoted on that small, slippery rock, placing his pack toward the pool, left leg still swinging in the air, weight shifting now backward toward the pool. I was now thinking, thank God. Freezing cold and wet would be much better than a crushed skull and twisted broken body.

I have no idea how or why, but he suddenly righted himself and simply hopped the remaining rocks to the safety of solid ground! We looked at each other in disbelief. Both gasping for air.

"How the hell did that happen?" I blurted, relieved that the dragging and phone call had been averted. "I thought you were dead! Really, I thought you were dead!"

"The minute I felt myself swaying, I used my pack weight to rebalance. I was never too far out of balance," Larry replied with a laugh. "I'm definitely getting new boots though."

I would like to tell you just how smooth and graceful Larry looked as he executed that stream crossing. Truth is, my daughter Sarah was once given a gift. A ridiculous gift. An entire set of the boy band - NSYNC- marionette puppets. I'm not kidding, she really did! I can still see Justin Timberlake, strings connected to strategic positions of the arms and legs and controlling cross sticks. Now, what kind of gift is that I ask you? Anyway, the point is, as you manipulated the cross sticks above old Justin, his legs would jerk and kick up in awkward motions as his arms flailed up and down like a wounded bird... That was what Larry looked like, dancing on that rock. He was Marionette Timberlake! Sorry Larry, I have to tell it like it is.

That hurdle cleared, we cinched up and headed down the final leg of our trip. We clearly hoped for no more crossings with such a degree of difficulty. The sun shone bright, the sky was clear blue, and the temperature continued to rise. We finished that mornings hike with nothing but ease and enjoyment.

What an eventful return to the mountains. We were impressed with this section of the Smokies. The trails were beautiful through this section. Our first December trip left us with some great memories. Hiking through old growth forest was a special experience. Our mouse buddy was not necessarily a trustworthy campmate. Minestrone soup was a fabulous food while riding out a deluge under a temporary shelter. High winds raging across an exposed bald were both exhilarating and debilitating. Hypothermia quickly took effect and pulled me down a spiral of physical inability and mental apathy. It was proven that a good hiking companion can be a life saver. Severe trials made for even sweeter success. At times, there was a blurry line between luck and skill. Adverse conditions actually went from miserably dangerous to strikingly beautiful.

It was good to be back.

Chapter 6
Twenty Mile Fail -
Walking Through History

I shouted to Dee, who was several yards ahead of me, "Look out, horses coming up behind us." She halted waiting for me to catch up. It was March and we had taken a few days for an Easter weekend backpacking trip in the Smokies. We had hoped to be married by now. This was supposed to be a honeymoon trip, but stuff happens and everything was postponed until July. Well, everything but this nature walk, Dee's first Smokies backcountry excursion.

Three horseback riders approached in a place where we could find little room to remove ourselves from their path. To our right was a bank rising steeply while the left was a precipitous drop. The trail here was rather muddy and narrow. The lead rider's mount balked as it neared us, rearing nervously, wide eyed, and head jerking. I must tell you that while Dee is extremely fond of just about all animals, she is a bit uneasy around horses. To her credit, we have gone riding with the kids on a few occasions and she saddled up with us, although somewhat uncomfortable with the idea, she rode with us. However, she felt quite threatened by this 1000 pound hoofed menace. The rider awkwardly dismounted, barley able to keep from falling over the drop. He quietly explained that pack burdened humans can spook horses. This was not a good place or time for that. We slippingly climbed a couple feet up the rise to our right and hugged the hillside as best we could. He attempted to lead his steed as it kicked, bucked, and jumped, flailing its head to the left wildly. Just as he reached us, the horse slipped off the trail, pulling his "rider" off the trail and over the edge. Disaster appeared to be imminent as the "rider" dug his boots into the hillside, pulling on the reins. The horse snorted loudly as he also frantically worked at reacquiring the trail. Dirt, plants and roots flew as he worked his way back up onto the path. The other two horses, while prancing somewhat nervously, maintained composure and solid footing. Once calmed, the lead horse was remounted and moved ahead, allowing the others to pass without incident. We all apologized for any problems caused, and all continued on their own way.

This being a heavily used horse trail, Dee was somewhat apprehensive about the possibility of other riders catching up to us, and repeat occurrences. Luckily such worries were unwarranted. Dee's first backcountry excursion was off to a great start! I have never had such an experience in the times I've been on the trail.

This was also my first Spring outing. The foliage was full and beginning to bloom, butterflies fluttered everywhere, the sun was shining. It was hot, and clouds of swarming gnats were everywhere! Did I ever mention that I liked to hike in the late fall and winter? We were sweating and as if on cue, whenever large volumes of air were needed, a cloud of those damned gnats would magically appear to be sucked into our throats, causing us to choke and gag. Welcome to pack life and the great outdoors, honey! I really know how to show a girl a good time!

We reached our camp #9 (Anthony Creek 3200') after a 3.8 mile trek. Right then and there we decided that this one night would suffice. That was Dee's inauguration into the world of backpacking. The next day we retraced our steps. Cades cove was crowed on that holiday weekend so we opted to base camp at Balsam Mountain. From there we explored a different section of the Smokies, doing shorter day hikes.

Two years later, we were now married and Dee was ready to give backpacking another try. We had been camping many times in the park's improved grounds over the last couple years and we decided Cades Cove would be on our route this time. I planned an ambitious route out of Twentymile Ranger Station in the southwest section of the park. The plan was to hike out of Twentymile in North Carolina, over the mountains and down into Cades Cove in Tennessee. Once there, we would hike the south side of the loop road, spend one night in Cades Cove Campground, then hike the other half of the cove loop road. Then we would return back over the mountain to our point of origination. Of course, we would spend several nights in the back country. The whole trip looked to be around 40 miles in 6 days.

As you read this you might be asking yourselves..."Do these people ever work?"

Trust me, all of us do have full time jobs. We just happen to have vacation and holiday time. Early on Dee and I decided that we would use these times to the fullest. By leaving after a final work day, and driving all night, we are able to squeeze trips in when many would not even try. Dee would often look at me and say, "I wish we could be..." Allow me to give you an example.

It was Thursday and we were eating lunch together, at work in Cleveland, Ohio, as we always did. Friday was a holiday, and the 3 day weekend sounded pretty good to us. It was a weekend we didn't have the kids. We were on our own. I asked what she would like to do for the weekend.

Dee looked at me and kiddingly said, "I want to watch the sunrise over the ocean at Myrtle Beach."

My reply was, "Well if we leave right after work we should be there just in time."

We rushed home after work and were packed and in the car, driving south 30 minutes later. We stood on the beach, 650 miles and 12 hours later, watching a beautiful sunrise over the breaking waves. Friday and Saturday were spent enjoying the shore before Sunday's drive home. That was not the first time and It has happened many times since, leading to varied destinations. Many times heading back home, we would drive all night, arriving just in time to shower and get back to our jobs on Monday morning. That's the way we worked it, fast and improvised! It did take a few days, and a lot of coffee to recover, but it worked for us. That phrase - "if we left right now" - became both a mood lightener, and often, a quick trip starter. It still is. I hope that clears the work thing up for you. Now we can get back to the trip at hand.

The nine hour drive to Twentymile Ranger Station proved to be dark, rainy, and exhausting. We squinted at the trailhead sign through the darkness as rain drummed on the car roof. We weren't really feeling it with the temp at 55 degrees, if you know what I mean. Fifteen minutes later we figured it was now or never.

"Let's suck it up and get moving," I offered. (I was trying to convince myself) "Once we stretch and get moving, things will feel better." (more of the same)

Donning rain gear, we checked the message board for any trail news or warnings, while filing our trip permit. All looked to be safe for travel. We put rain covers on our packs, stretched our muscles, hoisted our packs, and stepped onto the trail. While I tried to keep our pack weights to a minimum, extra food and other items had us heavier than I (I'm sure we) would have liked. We looked at a 1000' climb in the first three miles. The trail followed an old logging railroad bed. While Twentymile is a good trail, water was running in places due to the persistent rain. Just over 1.5 miles in we reached camp site #93 (Twentymile Creek 1880'). Packs dropped, we each took a handy stump for a badly needed rest. It continued to rain.

Each helped the other re-shoulder our burdens. Another 1.5 miles until we reach the junction with Long Hungry Ridge Trail. The trail was "coming to us" and our legs were doing their job. The rain continued and the trail was wet. Our plan was to take Long Hungry 4.6 miles to Gregory Bald Trail, Then 1.1 mile to #13(Sheep Pen). It would be a long day. Pushing hard, we reached the junction, dropped our packs and collapsed for another break. The rain had let up, so the Whisperlite was lighted. Soul warming vegetable beef soup performed its task. We felt better, and ready to continue on. Things were looking up.

Re-hitched, we hit Long Hungry Ridge. About a half mile later, things went south. Crossing Proctor Branch, Dee slipped on a wet rock, hell they were all wet. She strained her left upper hamstring. She was in obvious pain but did her best to pretend all was well. Knowing quite well that she was hurting, I attempted to assess her situation which she assured me, would be just fine. I got the message and left well enough alone. Within a mile we would reach another camp site. We could see how things looked then.

By the time we reached the site, she was in bad shape. I suggested we strongly consider turning back. Did I ever mention that my wife can be a bit stubborn? While I am the vision of open-mindedness and good sense,(now is when you roll your eyes) she does not give up easily. Tears welled in her eyes and she gave a stern no. She alluded to the fact that she didn't want to disappoint me, knowing how much I was looking forward to our endeavor. The obvious fact that her injury would not magically disappear over the next 35 miles, finally won out. She was terribly frustrated with the situation but it was what it was. Reluctantly she agreed to give up some of her load, to hopefully ease the return trek just a little.

We started our descent with her in the lead. It was going to be an uncomfortable 4 miles. Approaching Proctor Branch, (scene of the original crime) I cautioned Dee to take care. Wouldn't you know it, as I attempted to cross, my right foot slipped and I came down hard on my left foot. It felt like I completely collapsed my instep. The pain was excruciating. I probably did a little bit of the "marionette shuffle" myself, but with a painful landing.

Damn, that crossing physically messed both of us up. First half of the first day, and both of us were damaged goods. Must be what it's like being a Cleveland Browns first round draft pick (if you are a Browns fan you get it). Painfully we shuffled and limped our way back down the trail.

We were so happy as we approached the car. I was especially glad no one was there to witness our pathetic arrival. Even sliding into our seats was something of which to be ashamed. So much for our Twentymile exploit.

Once in the car, we did cut ourselves a little slack and actually laughed at our misery. We both found it fitting that Twentymile Trail was originally a rail bed, considering our trail bound "train wreck". The pressing question loomed...Now what do we do? We went there to camp and see Cades Cove and by golly, that's just what we were going to do.

Did you ever have your plans totally cave in, and still have the time of your life? The scenic drive around the southern end of the Smokies was a blast. Sure we were hurting physically, but we were seeing new sights, while resting our wounds. Restless Heart's Greatest Hits cassette had us singing and laughing as we rolled along. The song *Wheels* was our anthem in those days, and we sang away our pain. Damn, that was a great drive!

We followed route 28 back toward Fontana village. Our usual way of travel is to "feel" the area we are in. Simply stated, we wondered around, checking out whatever presented itself. Well, Fontana Dam presented, and we checked it out. Fontana Dam was way more impressive than I expected. At 480 feet high and 2365' long, it is an impressive sight. It was built within the years of 1942 - 1944, to impound the Tennessee River. This TVA hydroelectric dam forms Fontana Lake which boasts 238 miles of shoreline and 10,230 acres of surface. (TVA.gov) We had the dam to ourselves due to the late season and we limpingly enjoyed our time there. If you ever get the chance, check it out. We were pleasantly impressed.

It was time to find lodging for the night. We drove the back roads before finally spotting one those quaint older, mountain roadside motels. We were exhausted and ready to find a place to crash for the night. This small concrete block motel had a connected dinner. Damn - it was closed for the season. We noticed a light on and saw some movement inside. Being somewhat desperate, I knocked on the front doors of the dinner. To my surprise the woman who owned the motel opened the door and explained that they had just closed for the season. I explained that we just needed a room for the night. Southern hospitality is awesome! She opened a room, brought us bedding and towels. Unbelievable. We thanked her and she went about her business. I can't remember the name of that motel, but it is a fond memory. The room was nice clean and utilitarian. I parted the plastic curtain and stepped over the concrete entry to the shower. Not luxurious, but man I was glad to have it.

We had inquired as to the nearest place to eat. That was going to be another adventure. She eluded to the fact that there wasn't much open this time of year. Feeling the area, we went in search.

Several miles down the road, we spotted a small "rustic" plywood dining establishment. A lot of people I know would not have considered this an option. We did. We entered the one room dining area. A young lady stuck her head around the corner and motioned for us to seat ourselves. we took a corner table. The woman and her mother were friendly and went to work on our order. They gabbed and laughed as they worked their magic in the kitchen. You could see outside through gaps in the walls and spider webs decorated the corners. We viewed our decision as questionable. Soon a couple of groups came in, greeted us with gracious hellos and the eight of them gathered around a large table in the center of the room. Our food arrived, simple, southern fried, and pretty darn good. Our eight fellow dinners were obvious regulars. Their meals came out and they all joined hands and gave thanks. It was like being at family supper with a few friends. Rough and rustic...yes, friendly and relaxed...yes, worth the search and time...for sure. We said goodbye to our new acquaintances and left for our night's lodging feeling just a little enriched for our experience.

It was cold and dark when we pulled into the motel. I turned the wall mounted ceramic heater. We were plenty glad it worked. More Advil and we were asleep in no time. Hey, like I said, plans caved in on us. Although that day ended up completely different than planned, it was great after all.

The next morning we took a drive east through Cherokee and the Park on way to Cades Cove. We took our time checking out Climgmans Dome and several overlooks along the way. Traffic was minimal, and the drive was leisurely. Several hours of beautiful mountain travel put us back on track as to the middle part of the planned hike.

Cades Cove Campground was a welcome sight. We found a nice place to call home for a couple days. First things first...Advil was administered to the injured. We pitched camp and set about preparing dinner. We had plenty of backpack meals from which to choose. Pasta Primavera won out. That night we relaxed, licked our wounds, and savored our surroundings and good fortune. We hatched a genius plan over cups of coffee that night. We decided that, in the morning, we would drive our car to the visitor center at the far end of the loop road. There we would leave car, and hike the north half of the 11 mile loop back to our camp. The next day, hiking the south half would take us back to the car. That would be around 5.5 miles each day with light loads of water and a little food. We should be able to explore 6 homesteads, 2 churches and a water driven grist mill.

Sunrise found our car one of the first in line as the gates opened to loop road to traffic. Deer and turkeys could be seen as we drove quietly through the foggy morning air. We parked at the visitor center and checked out Cable Mill. Although there were other mills in the cove over the years, John P. Cable built his overshot waterwheel, the largest grist/lumber mill in the cove, in 1868. This is a well maintained piece of history, still operated by the park service April through October. (smokymountains.com)

We left the mill, and made our way toward the Elijah Oliver homestead. The going was already proving uncomfortable for both of us. Not to be deterred, we hobbled along, determined to hike through this historical "museum" as we originally intended. Elijah, the son of the original cove settlers, John and Lucrecia Oliver, had moved his family out of their first home (more on that later) and the cove, at the start of the civil war. They returned to the cove in 1865 and built this homestead. The buildings are off the road, a mile round trip excursion. What an amazing homestead. Elijah incorporated an "in home" spring house. Now that's quite a convenience for remote living in 1865. He also incorporated a "stranger room" for wayward travelers in need of temporary shelter (Cades Cove B&B). He Included a chicken coop, corn crib, and smokehouse, for an impressive family estate. We relaxed in the shade trying to imagine life at that time in this isolated cove, impressed with their ingenuity, craftsmanship, and self reliance.

Limping down the road, we headed toward our next stop. Next, we reached the Methodist Church. Established in 1820, but the building wasn't erected until 1902. The cemetery of over 100 graves was very interesting, and we found it worth our time. Both of these sites offered an inside look at social life in the cove.

We took a lunch break about half way between the church and our last stop of the day. The wisdom of this walking tour was now in question. We both underestimated the extent of our injuries. Dee could barely stride with her left leg and I was using my walking stick like a crutch. We loved the history, hated the "self- propelled tour bus". Reluctantly, we resumed our self-imposed, forced march.

The John Oliver homestead sits back in the upper end of a valley, about 1/4 mile from the road. The cabin is an impressive well-constructed structure. The interesting thing is, this really isn't John and Lucrecia's original cabin. The original cabin, built in the 1820s, which no longer exists, stood approximately 50 yards behind the current structure. The existing cabin was built in the 1850s as a honeymoon home for their son, Elijah, when he married. Elijah and his family, as mentioned earlier, left the cove, building a new homestead upon their return. John, Lucrecia and their decedents continued to use this cabin until the State of Tennessee took the land by condemnation in the early 1930s (NPSHistory.com). I have visited the Oliver homestead on several occasions. Looking up the valley at the land they cleared by hand, I can't help but admire the great courage, toil, and perseverance they expended, in building their life here. I recommend anyone interested in the history of the cove should read: *Cades Cove - The Life And Death Of A Southern Appalachian Community 1818-*

1937, by Durwood Dunn, it is a wonderfully, comprehensive insight, of the cove, its inhabitants, and community.

We reached our camp site, extremely sore, tired and hungry. Mac and cheese along with hot chocolate went down easily as we relaxed against a large tree. Reminiscing on today's sights, the history and beauty of the cove was more than worth the effort. And the fact that we completed at least a small portion of our original planned hike, did make us feel a little better about our overall fail. We were beat and unsure about tomorrow's hike. The idea of another day like today wasn't sounding either wise or enjoyable. Oh well, we decided to sleep on it. Tomorrow would be a new day. But for tonight, we painfully dragged ourselves into our tent.

Morning brought both rain and the realization that our "Cove" hike was over. Neither thought it wise to add to the extent of our injuries. With that decided, I was able to procure a ride to the visitor center and our waiting car.

That trip went nothing like we planned. The fact that we both ended up as walking wounded just a few hours after starting our journey, was both pathetic and disappointing. We did, however, keep an attitude of adventure and wonder, exploring Fontana Dam and the surrounding area, staying at a "closed" motel and eating in a friendly plywood diner. Cades Cove provided at least a partial hiking victory and an 1800's history lesson. Blown trip? Not in the slightest. We returned home feeling enriched, although somewhat hobbled, by it all.

Chapter 7

Steaks, Strikes, and Claustrophobia

Larry and I immediately started planning another trip in the northeast section as soon as we returned from our "Snake Den Ridge Tour of Hypothermia". Beautiful scenery and fewer people added up to exactly where, and when, we wanted to be. October or later would be our target time, as usual. Larry came up with another great loop, This time out of Big Creek. All new trails for 5 days and just over 31 miles. Big Creek would be our starting point. We were beyond ready to go when October 27 finally came.

Leaves of reds, oranges, golds and browns littered the trail. Right from the start, clear blue skies, sunny temperate weather, the smells and beauty of falling leaves, and the calming serenade of rushing mountain streams set the tone for a wonderful late Autumn outing. I've said it before, hitting the trail is one of the best feelings ever. Your existence on your back and nature all around you...if you have done it, you understand.

Big Creek Trail was extraordinary. Rushing mountain streams, boulders, pools, cascades- it was all there. We followed a fairly steady grade gaining around 1300' in 5.9 miles. The excitement of putting camp down in #36 (Upper Walnut Bottom 3040'), known for black bear activity, had all of our senses on alert. Encountering a bear in the wild was something we wanted to happen. The day passed pleasantly, with each bend of the trail revealing another view of the high surrounding ridges or tumbling stretches of clear flowing streams. All traces of family or work stresses just floated away on the gentle mountain breeze.

We reached Upper Walnut Bottom in mid afternoon. The area was broad, flat and ankle deep in fallen leaves. Tall trees surrounded us with a semi-bare canopy. The sky was cloudless blue. Dropping our packs, we laid back to enjoy the views, pleased with the lack of load and the knowledge that we were home for the night. Plans for the evening included the usual camp set up, a warm meal and laying out awaiting bruin company!

Having purchased a dehydrator, our dinner was our own concoction of rice, vegetables, including hot peppers, and spices. We hoped to equal that wonderful offering of 5 years earlier in the CCC Camp, by the light of our flaming socks. I had also purchased an MSR Whisperlite stove and we were taking it on its maiden voyage. It was a culinary success. A Three Musketeers Bar and cup of coffee or two in the advancing darkness added to our relaxed self-indulgence. It was a beautiful day indeed.

We awaited an evening visit. Laying out, enjoying the night sky as late as we could, to no avail. Sleep came...bears didn't.

As usual, we awoke with the very first dim light of day. As always we went about the morning chores, each taking care of one task or another. Drop and retrieve the food bag, set up stove and cook, replenish water supply, tear down and pack it all up. It still amazes me how effortless it is for us.

With everything packed and ready to roll, we looked over our map and trail guide, to orient ourselves for the day's travels. Gunter Fork Trail would lead us approximately 2000' in elevation gain over 4.1 miles. As it was in most cases, we were looking forward to heading to high ground.

It is rather hard to explain my need to get to high ridges as often as possible. Ever since that first time I packed across the high ridges off of Clingmans Dome, I have viewed high peaks and ridges as something I want to traverse. Driving down I77 through West Virginia and Virginia, I probably drive my family crazy pointing up to high forested spines, questioning what it would be like to be packing up there. I just can't help myself.

Anyway, another 1.4 miles on Balsam Mountain Trail would find our next camp in Laurel Gap Shelter at 5600'. And while we didn't relish the thought of spending the night in a mouse ridden enclosure, that was the likely outcome.

The morning was kind of typical of October in those mountains. Clear blue skies accompanied by temps in the mid 50s with an ever so slight breeze. Gunter Fork Trail was one of the best. Time and again we were treated to beautiful views of streams, pools, cascades and tumbling fast- water runs. Around 1.75 miles in, we came to a cascade of 150' or so drop. It also spread several feet across while splashing over and around jagged rocks and sliding over sloping smooth stone surfaces. The decision was made to break for a snack and some water while enjoying the stunning natural display. Slowly continuing our assent, we plodded on, breaking as needed. The crest of Balsam Mountain and trail junction was a welcomed place of rest and the perfect place for a warm pot of soup. We enjoyed a long leisurely break.

As the day wore on and altitude was gained, temperatures had slowly dropped, clouds steadily gathered, and the breeze gradually stiffened. I, of course, had hypothermia clawing at the back of my mind. Not fear, just a nagging reminder. That all vanished with the appearance of the shelter. Three stone walls, a roof, and a fireplace beckoned with its alluring promise of warmth and shelter.

The wind was starting to howl and snow started falling. Daylight was growing dim as we reached our domain for the night. When our reservation was made, others were registered for this site, so we weren't surprised to find two hikers already there. They had bunked at the far left end of the shelter which could house up to 14.

We shared cordial hellos but found them to be quiet and a bit standoffish. We judged them to be older (as compared to us in 1995), "speed hikers", as both wore knee supports, had double trekking poles, and meager gear. They were already preparing their evening meal by warming water for prepackaged Styrofoam cup of noodles. They stayed to themselves, talking quietly and turning in early.

It wasn't long before the blizzard hit! That howling wind was driving large snowflakes into our world at a furious pace. The ground was quickly covered as the snow continued to fall. We laughed as we threw our bags on upper middle bunks, glad to have beaten the weather gremlins to our shelter.

About then we were feeling a bit cocky as we set up to prepare our evening meal. Dehydrated potatoes, onions, garlic, peppers, snow peas and mushrooms sautéed in real butter should be the envy of those noodle eating elders, we were sure. We just got the butter in the pan when out of nowhere 2 male hikers burst into the shelter out of the blizzard. We nodded our greetings just as 2 female hikers and another male entered, laughing and shaking off their snow covered clothes and gear. By now 2" of the white stuff covered the ground.

We continued our culinary endeavors as the college age newcomers began to settle in. They asked if any of us minded a fire. They went out to gather wood with our good blessings. A couple of them commented on the wonderful smell coming from our stove and we offered to share with all that might desire. They thanked us, assuring that they intended to use the fire for their own preparations.

These five were quite different from our other two campmates. They freely talked and laughed as they made themselves comfortable and stoked the fire. We were enjoying good conversation with our mates as we dined on our gourmet meal.

Larry looked me at and laughed as they started pulling out their rations. Two inch thick steaks, baking potatoes the size of softballs, corn on the cob, and of course, a few bottles of wine! Oh to be young. We assured them that they really knew the ropes of proper backpacking. We all had a good laugh.

Little things can bring about fond memories and warm feelings. And it is different for each one of us. Both Larry and I are big baseball fans. Cleveland Indians fans in particular. We have been fans through some of the worst years of Cleveland baseball ever. The 60's sucked...the 70's sucked...the 80's sucked...and still we listened on the radio, watched on TV and went to some games at that old cavernous 74,000 seat ball park, called Cleveland Municipal Stadium. We have our heroes like, Sam McDowell, Louis Tiant, Duke Sims, Rocky Colavito, Chico Simone, Duane Kuiper, Larry Brown. You've probably never heard of most of these guys. Am I right? That's what being an Indians fan was about in those days. Heck, we could drive 50 miles after work, buy a ticket and sit anywhere we wanted. I remember more than one game sitting in our favorite upper deck box seats on the 3rd base line with a few hundred of our closest friends! No kidding... 74,000 seats and 1000 or less fans. You could hear the guy on the other side of the stadium ask for a beer! Now those are fond memories.

Anyway, it just so happened that the Indians, our Indians, were playing in the final game of the World Series against the Atlanta Braves on this very night. The first time in the Series since 1954! I was prepared. I had a small portable AM radio on top of that mountain, just hoping we could pull in the game. Being considerate bunkmates, we ask our fellow shelter dwellers if they would mind if we tried to tune in the game. No dissenters. As a matter of fact, the late comers were all college students from Georgia and were Braves fans.

What a night. The smell of fire roasted steak, corn and potatoes, the wine was flowing and believe it or not...KMOX out of St. Louis was coming in sporadically! We all bonded just a little that night. We nodded in and out along with the fluxing radio waves and flickering flames of the fire. In the end the Indians lost that final game 1-0. All in all, a very special memory that would be hard to imagine, if it hadn't really happened. But it did.

Later that night while all were sleeping soundly, due to fatigue and for some, partially due to the wine, another memorable moment occurred. It was very cold as the fire died out and I decided to take full advantage of my mummy sleeping bag. For those not acquainted with mummy bags, I offer this - Proper use of a mummy bag demands complete encasement within the bag. An attached hood also surrounds your head leaving only your face exposed, for breathing purposes of course. There are zipper pulls inside the bag allowing for closure from within. Once inside, body heat is entrapped ensuring a warm and restful sleep.

Unless, that is, you suddenly awake and feel restrictions at the shoulders and hips, hands and arms, unable to move freely, and an attack of acute claustrophobia strikes! In that case you awake as if buried alive in a coffin! Yep, I'm claustrophobic...yep, I panicked...yep, I couldn't find that damned inside zipper pull to save my ass...yep, I was trying to un sheath my knife to cut my way out...yep, I was flopping around like a fish out of water... yep, Larry was trying to talk me down from the ledge (quietly), as he grabbed for my furiously flopping zipper pull...yep he un-cocooned me in the nick of time. My heart rate slowed, and my breathing returned to some normalcy. Wow, that hit me without warning. I should have known that might happen, but I felt so proudly in control as I zipped myself in originally. Pathetic. If anyone else heard my cowardly struggle, they kept it to themselves. Covering myself loosely, (screw that damn zipper), I eventually returned to sound, calm, though somewhat colder slumber.

Most of the previous day's snow was blown from the camp and trail during the night. First light came, windless along with a slightly warmer temperature. With oatmeal, coffee, and packing out of the way, we said our goodbyes to the two lone Georgians that were awake at the time. The speed trekkers had lit out a few minutes before us, poles quickly keeping time with their hurried pace. We ambled off at our usual leisurely gait.

Our day would consist of 9 miles with a lot of downhill leading to camp #39 (Pretty Hollow 3040'), a heavily used horse camp. We, of course, hoped to camp alone in this quiet valley with a close by water source. Our morning passed without incident. Mild temps and cloudy skies aptly describe the day. While eating lunch, a Park Ranger (a rare sight in the backcountry) strode up and took time to break with us. He warned of a somewhat aggressive bear at camp

#39 the previous night. He urged caution, as this particular animal seemed quite difficult to discourage from camp raiding. We expressed our concern and thanked him for the information.

Yahoo! We were so excited. This would be our chance to see a bear for sure. We pressed on with a renewed vigor. Further down the trail, we met three fellow packers. They inquired as to our destination for the night. They warned us about the bear at #39. They were camped there the night before and had lost some food and had tent damage due to the furry marauder. Their account painted the bruin as fiercely aggressive and very persistent. Another site was their sincere suggestion.

Sweet! This was a sure thing! We couldn't wait. It was finally going to happen. The last half of our day was a pleasant downhill stream side hike, heading into the valley. Reaching #39 a little later than our normal camp arrival, we set to the task establishing camp. We cautiously prepared and ate dinner a little farther away from our camp than usual. We carefully hung our packs and food on the provided cables.

Each gathered a good supply of appropriately sized rocks to be used as deterrent ammunition if needed. A log to lean on, pots to bang on, rocks at hand, and a hot cup of coffee was all we needed for an exciting evening of bear adventure. We waited patiently. We waited patiently some more. We waited patiently a little longer. Now we waited impatiently. Damn it... how could this happen. A perpetrator with a red hot recent rap sheet. The perfect scenario.

No Show!

Crawling into our tent, we were extremely tired and disappointed but a bit apprehensive. I pictured a large, aggressive, hungry, angry bear ripping our tent to shreds and dragging out two "pigs in a blanket" for a late night mauling. Oh, that was an unsettling thought. Sleep came restlessly.

That morning we awoke after an uneventful night, resigned to the realization that wildlife interaction would never be in our cards.

Come to think of it, that is not really true. A few years back we were backpacking out of Cades Cove. After visiting Gregory Bald, we put down camp in #13 (Sheep Pen Gap). There we met a lone trekker named Mark. He was an interesting guy with stories of thru hiking the Appalachian Trail the previous year. We invited him to have beef stew with us and he was happy to join us as long as he could provide dessert. I added a small extra tarp as a patio in front of our tent for entertaining our guest. We had a great time sharing stories over stew followed by Mark's brown sugar and cinnamon Pop-Tarts with coffee. Mark retired to his camp and we turned in. We were startled awake by a guttural growling accompanied by a ripping/crackling sound. With superhuman reactions I grabbed my headlamp, unzipped the tent and looked out in time to glimpse a coyote running downhill with my small "patio tarp" trailing behind him. I yelled and chased him, in my stocking feet, slipping and sliding on the dry fallen leaves. Terrified by my menacing presence, he left the "patio" behind and sprinted off into the night, his attempted camp raid defeated. Mark and Larry joined me upon my arrival back at the tent. We all had a good laugh as I remembered that I had dropped a small bit of stew on the now coyote tooth perforated tarp, the sure cause of the night raid.

Now I feel better...animal interactions are a possibility.

Our day was cut out for us. We were heading up and in just 5.1 miles we would climb 2780' ending on the summit of Mount Sterling. Weather permitting, the views from the peak would be fabulous. The night sky promised to be spectacular. The day was mostly sunny and warmer than we expected. It proved to be a tough day with plenty of sweat. Just short of 4 miles in, we reached the junction with Mount Sterling Ridge Trail. Dropping our gear, we collapsed, glad to be done with Pretty Hollow Gap Trail's steady climb. My legs were pretty darn tired and I was already wishing to be lounging on the summit.

The 1.4 miles of Mount Sterling Ridge trail had way too much up then down, just to go up again. Not to my liking. As I said, my legs were already telling me to rest, way too often. When we reached the sign for the Mount Sterling trail I gladly shucked it all and laid down, wishing it was done. Only a half mile to the summit. Now we were talking.

Son of a gun...that half mile was a long way! My legs fought me every inch of that steep damned stretch! By the ever increasingly steep end, I was stopping every three to four steps to rest my legs and suck air. My heart leaped with joy and I slumped with relief as we reached the peak, and viewed that lovely abandoned 60' fire tower. Halleluiah!

It was with great sadness and much whining that we hiked downhill .4 miles then down a 700' side trail in order to replenish our depleted water supply at a small spring. Canteens and water bottles full, we now had to climb back up to camp. Pitiful to see grown men cry.

That night we camped a few feet from the base of the tower, under the brightly twinkling night stars. It was quite cold and breezy on that peak, and we loved every minute of it. About 9 o'clock we decided to climb that old tower for an extended view. The tower has steps with 4 landings leading to the locked observation cabin 60' up. I shakily halted on the first landing, feeling my unwanted fear of heights take hold. I hate my phobias.

For instance, on that trip to Canada right after high school graduation, (mentioned earlier), I had a battle with the height thing. We were pretty much in the middle of nowhere, 400 miles north of the border. My buddy was quite familiar with the area, due to previous fishing trips with his dad. He wanted to take us to, you guessed it, an abandoned fire tower on top of a mountain, 20 miles from our cabin. We drove down dirt roads for miles. At one point the road was completely washed out to the depth of 3 feet. We got out of the car and piled rocks up in front of the wheels in order to cross the wash. It worked and we drove on up to the tower. It was pretty cool. An old abandoned stone ranger cabin and the 80' tower. My two buddies climbed up the ladder and into the observation cabin through the opened trap door. Yes, this tower had a ladder instead of stairs. I climbed about half way up and totally froze. I mean arms wrapped completely around the ladder and I couldn't move! They yelled for me to join them for the unbelievable view. I shakily explained my inability to do so. That's when the never ending abuse started. Wow, they really laid it on. Then they started down the ladder. They threatened to jump up and down on my shoulders if I didn't get my ass down. This went on way too long. Finally I somehow forced myself shakily down to the wonderfully stable earth.

My God, they were relentless with insults and name calling. Once back to the cabin, they decided to take the boat out fishing. Thoughtfully they offered to tie me to a tree to save me from fear of boating. I politely told them where that boat should be stored and off they went.

I decided right then and there that I would climb that tower or die trying. I grabbed the keys and drove agitatedly toward the tower. Luckily I made it across our rock tire paths and to that damn tower. I grabbed onto that ladder and started climbing. After making the mistake of looking out at the scenery about half way up, I refocused on the ladder in front of my face the rest of the way. I crawled through the trap door and stood upright in victorious elation. I walked over to the windows and screamed loudly for my two good friends to go F... well you might be able to guess what I had to say.

They were right, the view was breathtaking. I memorized some of the graffiti on the interior walls as proof of my conquest. I did find it a bit difficult easing down through that trap door and reacquiring a foothold on the ladder. But I did and the rest was history.

For quite some time I was cured of that phobia. It does come and go. I just take it as it comes.

Well, back on Mount Sterling (5820'), the view was really good from my landing and according to Larry, even better at the top.

Once back in our beds, stars bright and wind whistling creepily through the towers super structure, we enjoyed our night atop Sterling.

All in all it was a another great trip. The trails, streams, cascades and pools were top notch. Once again bad weather turned into an extraordinary event. Our usual loathing of strangers in shelters gave way to a friendly, enjoyable evening with college kids doing it their own way. Even a World Series loss is kinda special when heard from a little radio crackling and hissing with interference on a cold windblown mountain top. Caution must be exercised when claustrophobic and sleeping in a mummy bag. I have too many phobias. Bears are unpredictable. Once again, steep long uphill days are difficult when one is out of shape. High peaks with great views are worth steep long uphill days.

Chapter 8
The Rabbits

We were back in Ohio and brewing a batch of stout while reminiscing over our last Smokies outing. Once again the smells of combined malt and hops churning together in our brew pot had our senses tingling with excitement. The dark roasted steeping grains added another layer of intensity to the always tantalizing aromas of the brew day kitchen. We both raised our mugs for another draw of our latest brew, an Irish stout that we rated as very good.

"Why don't we try to get our boys out for their first backpacking trip this Spring?" Larry threw out.

"They are pretty young and we would have to outfit them. But we should be able to plan a good trail they can handle. That would be really cool."

My son, Justin was 12 and Larry's son, Matt was 10. We figured it was about time for them to give it a try. Both had tent camped before, but neither had backpacked.

"Maybe their Spring break would work," Larry said.

We clinked our mugs and I hurried to retrieve our well worn trail map.

And so the process began anew!

We had "car camped" with all of the kids at times. My wonderful wife, Dee and I had taken Justin and my daughter, Jaclyn on many excursions. They had tent camped during our many rock hounding forays in Arizona, Montana, South Dakota, Ohio, North Carolina, Utah, Nevada, Kentucky, New Mexico, and Canada. They were no strangers to improved campgrounds or out in open country. Having a wife that enjoys roughing it as well as searching and digging in the dirt for gem and mineral specimens is truly a blessing to this man of varied and quirky interests. Life with her is very much an adventure that I treasure.

Larry and I thought giving our two sons a chance at the trail, with their own gear on their backs would be exceptional. Three to five days on the trail could be possible. Many ideas were kicked around. High ridges, good views, less strenuous trails, wildlife, old homesteads, all taken into account. We wanted them to fondly remember this trip, not hate it as fatherly administered torture. A water bottle, their clothes, a sleeping pad, and possibly a sleeping bag would be all they would carry. We did not want to overload them. The whole trip would be geared to their enjoyment. So we hoped.

Cades Cove was the decided destination. Old cabins and other historic structures would lend considerable interest. Gaining Gregory bald should yield great views. Possible elk, bear, turkey, deer, and wild boar sightings, added exciting anticipation.

The boys were stoked when we told them our plans. An all guys road trip! They well knew that meant real adventure. Because, dads of course do things a little differently (read as: somewhat goofy and at times just a little reckless).

I had everything Justin needed, including Dee's pack which fit him very well. Larry bought a small internal frame pack for Matt. I can't lie to you, Larry and I were probably more excited than the boys. We couldn't wait to share the wonders of trail living with them. We hoped they could only feel the same spiritual connection with the mountains that we've treasured so many times. We knew it would be a balancing act between getting them to exciting terrain, within physical reason and going too far, making backpacking their idea of hell on earth. One man's heaven may not be his son's. For instance...

A few months earlier, Dee and Justin both decided to take the hunters education course. I went with them to the classes and we all enjoyed attending together. They both earned their license.

I had been constantly talking of my wonderful time in nature while squirrel hunting. I of course would hit the woods in the early morning darkness, settle in against a tree, watching and listening as the forest awoke. Deer happened by, birds of all types began moving and singing their melodies. Small rodents scurried in their daily chores, at times using me as a byway. As first light barely illuminated the high tree tops, the movements of squirrels, gathering their winter food stores or leaves for insulating their nests, captured my attention. I would spend hours as motionless as possible, observing it all. Many times without firing a shot, content as a forest observer. It was not unusual for a deer or two to walk and feed within a few feet of me, or to have a bird land on the barrel of my flintlock. Squirrels have also descended the tree I rested against within inches of my shoulders before realizing a retreat might be wise. All of this brings me comfort and feeds my soul.

Justin was more inclined to lay in his sleeping bag and read a comic while waiting for me to alert him of any squirrelly actions. The act of hunting never became an activity he enjoyed. Especially the harvesting of a living animal. I respect his conscious decision and certainly had no problem with that. Just a difference of desires and interests.

The point being, I hoped carrying a load while living in the woods for a few days with no plumbing or even a port-a-pot as items of comfort (what the hell am I saying), would be an adventure to be cherished, and not a torment of their young minds and bodies.

We were a bit more concerned about Matt carrying a load, as he was younger and physically smaller. But, he was game and ready to go. So, Larry worked out his "loading formula".

We cautiously considered our meal choices. Delicious foods to keep energy and satisfaction at high levels were a must. Soups, stews, snacks, eggs, pancakes, and hot chocolate were on the menu. We carried quite a lot of everything. We knew these boys could eat and we amply prepared.

This meant Larry and I would be carrying extra everything including water. Our pack weights ballooned to levels not desired but necessary just the same. That was that. Come March we would be on our first father/son backpack expedition.

March, 30 at 1am we were all in the van and off toward Gatlinburg, TN., gateway to the Smokies. It didn't take long for Justin and Matt to fall asleep. They remained comatose pretty much the whole trip until we woke them somewhere in Tennessee for breakfast at Bob Evans. We figured that would be a pleasant boost for them both mentally and physically. They took full advantage!

Both boys thought Pigeon Forge appeared to possess all of the amusement and tourist wonders of the world. Perhaps we should just adventure there for a few days? I thoughtlessly drove on. The Sugarlands Visitor Center offered its own bit of excitement with varied visual displays of wildlife (especially bears), peaks and waterfalls. Our backcountry permits were also submitted.

That stop completed, Cades cove with its many visible cabins, and a visitor center of its own, was the next objective. A few souvenirs and a new trail guide book in hand, we pressed on. Driving part of the loop road, we pointed out some of the cabins and outbuildings, impressing the historic importance of this settlement on our two young, somewhat distracted sons. Backwoods trails were calling.

Unfortunately, rain fell on and off as we drove toward our destination. We knew the weather would be iffy, and it was what it was. Parking at the Visitor Center, the boys geared up. Rain suits, packs with rain covers, of course, and walking sticks, completed their attire. The first day entailed a 600' gain in elevation over 3.9 miles. We figured that to be a reasonable first day.

Right away we learned it would be a challenge keeping those two in sight. Several times we called to them over and over, only to find them restlessly waiting for us quite a way ahead, up the trail. We explained the dangers and ease of veering off the main trail, losing both their way and contact with us. It was here they became known as "The Rabbits".

Justin, of all people should have known and understood that concept. Let me explain.

About a year earlier, Dee and I brought Justin and Jaclyn to the Smokies for a weekend in Cherokee. We drove through the night and started up 441. The road crests at Newfound Gap just over 5000'. We encountered freezing rain as we gained altitude. It was an extremely tenuous drive. We barely made it to New Found Gap at around 4am. We stopped and kicked back for some rest, glad to be alive and hoping the weather would improve before heading down the eastern side of the mountain.

We were awakened out of a sound sleep by the friendly knocking on my window. I drowsily lowered my heavily fogged window, bidding a good morning to the attending park ranger. In a not so friendly tone, we were told we couldn't sleep there and that we needed to get up and moving. Unimpressed by my explanation of the night's freezing rain and overall unsafe driving conditions, - "wake up and get moving" - was emphatically restated. And so we did.

Our doors were opened to a very chilly but promisingly pleasant looking morning. With Justin and Jaclyn, now up and moving, we all headed to the restrooms, which were located down a paved pathway below the parking lot. Back at the van we prepared a gourmet breakfast of juice and granola bars. We sat on the wall overlooking the gap road as it wound its way down towards Cherokee, North Carolina.

Hoping the road to Clingmans Dome was now clear of snow and ice, we cleaned up and put away the sleeping bags as we prepared to see an early morning view from the peak. It was then that we realized Justin was not there. Jaclyn, Dee and I all looked at each other hoping one of us knew his whereabouts. No one did. We began calling him expecting he would pop from the other side of the overlook wall. Not there. Dee asked the few others who had recently arrived, to no avail. I went back to the restrooms...not there. We were now panicking. I ran up the path to the top of the Rockefeller Memorial...no Justin.

Dee and Jaclyn stayed with the van hoping he was close by while I tried the only other idea we could come up with. The Appalachian Trail passed through and was just above the parking lot. I ran to the trail and headed up the steeply climbing trail to the south. I ran as fast as I could while calling his name and quickly looking over any drop-offs. About 3/4 of a mile up the trail I was bent over gasping for air when a couple came walking down the trail. I inquired if they had seen a young boy in a red flannel shirt on the trail. They had and even asked him why he was alone on the trail. He assured them all he was ok. I thanked them and resumed my running search, relieved to know I was at least on the right track.

About another 1/4 mile further up the trail, we met as he was now walking back toward the parking area. Even though I could hardly breathe at that point, I strongly implored as to the error of his ways. It was a strange mix of total relief, parental anger, and breathless exhaustion with which I walked back to the van. Dee and Jaclyn finally relaxed when we appeared fully intact.

Justin on the other hand was quite upset with my adverse reaction to his epic feat. His effort was only a way to show us that he could hike the trail, just as we would. I of course negatively pointed out that the trail would have continued to take him clear to Georgia! Happy ending, but not my finest moment.

You get the point.

Back to our story, all 4 of us finally made it to site #12 (Forge Creek 2600'), together. The weather was cool but dry for now. Fathers and sons erected tents. Water was filtered and supper was quickly prepared. We figured beef stew would be a welcomed meal for their first night on the trail, and it was devoured readily. Cups of coffee and hot chocolate would finish off the evening. The boys broke out the deck of cards ready for a father, son euchre game. For the next hour or so, cards and laughs were flying around our tight little circle, illuminated by our headlamps. It sure was fun sharing the experience together. Bushed, we crawled into our trailside abodes for a well- deserved night's rest.

It was at that point that Larry first voiced his misgivings on his choice of tents. He had recently purchased a new, small, two- man tent for weight and size savings. Now, in actual real trail circumstances, lack of headroom and total space made for cramped quarters. However, fatigued, both Matt and Larry quickly nodded off in their nylon "tiny house".

Now, on the other hand, Dee and I bought a Eureka Glacier Bay 2 man tent, while attending the Ohio Sportsman's Show a year earlier. It packed small and light while offering a small vestibule. It easily housed Justin, I and our equipment. We were quite comfortable.

Morning dawned dreary, cool and foggy. Coffee, hot chocolate, pancakes and scrambled eggs lightened our dispositions. We tore down camp, packed and rigged for the trail.

It almost immediately became apparent that we had underestimated the difficulty of this trail. Steep grades and sharp switchbacks were the obvious order of the morning. Both boys were struggling under their loads. Honestly, I was too. The views were a bit hazy but gave us reason for numerous breaks. About the 2nd switchback, Matt gave up and Justin was also burning out fast. No Rabbits here! We urged them to enjoy the view while Larry and I evaluated our dilemma. I took on Justin's water load and Larry ended up with Matt's entire pack. I tried to convince Larry to split more of the load with me. He insisted he would tow the load.

All together this day would demand 4.6 miles and 2400' in elevation gain. Perhaps we miscalculated during our planning sessions. I seem to do that way too often. Slowly we stumbled on. Once again the movie *The Treasure of Sierra the Madre* comes to mind. I envision Humphrey Bogart and Tim Holt (Dobbs and Curtin), several days into their prospecting expedition in the remote Mexican mountains. Both men while driving their pack mules up the mountain side, stumble and collapse, overheated, overtaxed, sweat stained, and ready to throw in the towel. Loaded like the pack mules, spiritless like Dobbs and Curtin, amen... that was us.

We were relieved to find a relatively level section a mile further up the trail. We laid back for another well deserved break after dropping our gear. Man, flat ground looked so good. We feasted on granola, jerky and water, food of the gods. Rested and replenished, we readied to push on. Matt grabbed his pack, much to Larry's relief. Old "Burning Knees" was glad for the reprieve. Everyone geared up and off we went, each under his own load.

The boys trudged on, encouraged by the promise of spectacular views from Gregory Bald. Miles faded slowly but finally the trail opened into a well worn path through a grassy hillside. We made it to the bald!

Oh no...after all the buildup and hype we fed them for incentive to forge ahead...nothing but fog. The disappointment was all too evident.

I've only seen this kind of discouragement on these guy's faces one other time.

A year after this trip, I suggested a pack trip in the Black Forest Trail in central Pennsylvania. Hills, valleys. streams and overlooks were all inducements. I also dangled a carrot in way of The Black Forest Inn, which we would encounter halfway through our trek. While packing this trail a few years earlier, Dee and I happened onto the Inn. Great rustic atmosphere, cold birch beer and the most phenomenal mushroom swiss burger ever! Anyway, after a hot 2nd day of hiking we approached the promised land! Everyone was ready for that cold birch beer, and the coveted burger. It couldn't be...the damned place was closed for renovations! Same kind of mutinous facial expressions were now being displayed on Gregory Bald.

Larry and I did our best to console the disenchanted duo. After all, we too were not exactly pleased with the lack of scenery. We waited a short time hoping for an opening in the shroud. No luck. The possibility of seeing a wild boar was our positive enticement to placate the depressed pair. We had seen much sign the last time we visited the intended camp, #13 (Sheep Pen Gap). Yes, also the scene of "The Great Coyote Stewed Tarp Caper"! Anything would be possible.

Increasing drizzle and dropping temperatures dictated a quick camp set up and we hurriedly completed dinner. We retired to our tents early. Rhythmic drumming of light rain tapping on our rain flies provided a musical backbeat.

Each tent broke out the cards for evening entertainment. Justin was on his game and the action in our tent was fast and furious. We laughed and slammed down hand wining cards with command. Our close fought game was suddenly interrupted.

"This sucks," Larry shouted. "Shut up over there."

"What's your problem?" I answered his demand.

"This damn tent is so low, we can't even lay on our sides, up on our elbows, without hitting the ceiling. And the temps are dropping and it's so tight in here condensation from our breath is dripping on us. To top it off, you two are over there partying in your Glacier Bay "mansion," He explained tongue in cheek.

"You can use our guest quarters if you like," I answered in my best mansion dweller voice. "It is definitely getting cold. Hope you can at least get some sleep and stay warm."

Justin and I continued our game with a little more reserve, in respect to their crappy situation. In short order we finished up for the night and drifted off to sleep.

We woke up at first light to a cold damp morning. It was a misty 34 degrees. Like I said, we knew the weather for this trip would be questionable but it had to be now or never when we planned it. In our usual mindset we figured we could take it.

Larry and Matt had little good to say about their tent. They were cramped and water droplets continued to provide Chinese water torture throughout the night. At one point Matt had woken Larry concerned about the wild boar he heard very close to their tent.

"For God's sake...that's your uncle Jeff snoring!"

"That can't be human," Matt answered.

"Oh yes it is. I've heard that ridiculous sound enough to know."

Whiners.

We savored breakfast with the customary hot beverages and its internal heating properties. We were eager to get packing, knowing the movement induced warmth would be a welcomed effect. We would be heading down Gregory Bald trail, descending 2000' over the next 4 miles. We could then break at the junction with Parson Branch Road.

Within the first mile a heavy wet snow began to cover the trail. The wind had picked up and conditions were not the best. But, the boys were enjoying the adventure of a snowy mountain descent, to our great relief. These two were as delusional as their fathers!

About three miles into the day, at around 3000', the snow changed to a heavy downpour. Temperatures had risen to the mid 40s and conditions deteriorated to miserably unhealthy at best.

Parson Branch Road was a welcomed sight indeed. Wet, cold and shivering, we quickly threw up a tarp for shelter against the chilling downpour. We rested under its sheltering canopy, and assessed our progress. A steaming pot of minestrone soup seemed a necessary aid at that point. With a spin of our Bic lighter's striking wheel, the Wisperlite hissed to life. As the pot simmered, Larry and I quietly discussed our options.

The weather report was sounding quite negative for the foreseeable future. We would have around 4.4 miles to go today, ending at site #14 (Flint Gap). We would then have two more days and one night, all possibly in similar rainy conditions. The alternative being, hike out Parson Branch Road to Forge Creek Road and back to the car. Probably around five miles. Larry and I agreed that would be the best case scenario but decided to lay out the options and let the boys decide.

Warming just a little with each spoonful of that savory blend, we explained the two choices. We then left it up to them. Our immediate fate was in their hands. I should add that we did mention a hotel with dry beds and steak dinner to option number two, just for clarification. Neither wanted be the one to wimp and call for the bailout. You could see the anguish on both of their faces but they refused to cave.

Being the responsible fathers that we are, Larry and I both voiced the opinion that the bailout looked to be perhaps, the more prudent of the options. Justin and Matt instantly concurred after hearing our wise input. Decision made, we hurriedly downed the minestrone, packed our gear, and plunged back into the deluge.

Parson Branch Road is an eight- mile gravel road running from Cades Cove to Highway 129. There are 18 creek fords in this stretch. It is often closed to traffic due to storm damage, high water, and always closed in winter. At that particular time it was closed due to extensive storm damage.

The "Rabbits" were loose and on the run. We cautioned them to stay within sight but a straight shot road ending at our van, led us to ease up on the reins just a bit. The clouds continued their assault as we ambled soggily down the road, or river, if you will. This byway was running, ankle deep at times. And to add insult to injury, downed trees...very large downed trees...blocked our progress often. Climbing over, climbing under, or detouring off-road and around were all techniques employed at one time or another. Oh, how youth made those endeavors appear much easier than Larry and I found them to be!

At this point, Larry came to the, too late, conclusion that waterproof hiking boots were a good idea. While my feet were relatively dry, Larry might as well have been hiking with feet wrapped in Kleenex! His shoes were a waterlogged limp mess and his feet suffered for it. As we rested on a downed tree, he vowed his first plan of action, once home, to be the research and purchase of a pair of remedies to this malady.

Matt and Justin were waiting beside the van when we got there. They both were laughing and joking as they snacked on candy bars, drenched but happy. We all stripped as much soggy clothing as modestly possible before entering our awaiting coach. Due to the aforementioned conditions and obstacles, the Parson Branch ordeal took over three hours to complete. All involved, no worse for wear, found great joy in the fact that warm dry beds and a like dinner table were just down the road.

I do believe the boys were more than pleased with their choice to bail as we wound our way through the valleys and out of the park. Four pairs of eyes scanned closely for places of lodging and good food as we drove through Gatlinburg. Of course, inexpensive was the main criteria as to our preference of lodging. While scouting motels, a few promising restaurants caught our attention.

"There it is" I pointed to the sign which offered rooms for $21. Vacancy was the second item of notice.

A clean room with 2 queen beds welcomed us as I opened the door to our castle. Warm showers and dry clothes would be the first order. Justin was the first to shower and he found a wall mounted heater in the bathroom. Of course he turned it to the high setting. Noting that it was the only source of heat in the room, it remained on as we left for meat and potatoes. Clean, dry and warm, we were now four hungry men of the woods.

We spotted a most promising establishment as we retraced our earlier drive through town. There, looking through the continuing downpour, was a restaurant with a large circular fireplace, all aflame, and calling to us..."come, sit by the fire, partake of a steak as big as your head, oh yes, don't forget to have a beer". That was our kind of calling. You are right of course...cold, wet, strenuous activities do tend to add to my delusions!

Soups, salads, steaks, baked potatoes and a roaring fire, made us whole again. Watching the cold rain drenching everything outside of our cozy refuge, we patted ourselves on the back for such wise decision making. We stretched that meal out as long as we could, not wishing to leave the provided comforts. As all good things must come to an end, we said our farewells and left the restaurant which we still fondly remember.

Upon our return to our room for the night. Opening the door something smelled very hot. Cautiously entering, we wisely checked out the bathroom heater. You could hardly touch the wall! Damn that thing was hot. Turning it off, we were glad we had not been gone a minute longer or the motel may have combusted into a cinder pile. Catastrophe avoided and room comfortably warmed. That's a win, win!

Just a side note - We have learned, after many such negative occurrences, that Justin should never be trusted with heating or cooling controls of any kind! I embrace that principle to this day.

Having our sons with us made for a different trip. Lessons were learned. Fathers, at times, tend to expect too much out of young sons. Conversely, fathers, at times, don't give their young sons enough credit. I can't say enough about sharing the joys, discomforts, accomplishments, fun, discoveries, and camaraderie of the trail with them. Steep trails fraught with pain and minor setbacks brought about sacrifices, excruciating efforts, and ultimately, teamwork and accomplishment. Weather, as so many times before, dealt some disappointing blows, providing seemingly negative conditions only to enhance our sense of adventure in the end. Cheating ourselves out of several more days on the trail, gave us the chance to encourage educated decision making, and the willingness to accept alternatives to premade plans. A nice fire, good steak, large beer or hot chocolate, and good companions can trump an early departure. It was a pleasure for these two old dogs to run with the Rabbits.

Chapter 9

Three Generations and Still No Fish

L arry, Justin, and I headed to Clingmans Dome for a trip in October of that same year. We traveled 29.5 miles over 5 days on the trail. It was another great trip. Fall was once again, beautiful in the Smokies. We encountered very few hikers in our camps (thumbs up), and star gazing was fantastic. Justin advanced his trail savviness, and we became a trail trio elite. We traveled well, ate very well, and had many rousing three- handed euchre games. It was an enjoyable journey with great weather, clear skies, rippling streams, and injury-free trekking. It went so smoothly that these pages wouldn't find much of noteworthy content.

Well, Larry did renew a proclivity mentioned earlier in this book...the constant singing of a song. This trip, *Strawberry Wine* by Deana Carter could not be quieted. My God, it was never ending. He couldn't explain the strange affliction. It would just instinctively flow out of Larry like someone had opened a faucet. We all found it to be annoyingly entertaining.

The last day did give us some fodder. Morning was dark and we hurriedly broke camp to get an early start. We had around three miles and a 2000' climb as our morning walk. Just as we prepared to head out, it began to rain. We quickly draped a tarp over us hoping a quick passing shower would soon be over. Nope...soon water made its way under our tarp and seating became damp at best. We folded the tarp and strapped everything to our packs for the morning's climb. Justin decided to take a cut of the tent in order to ease my load for the coming climb. I gratefully accepted his offer.

Justin had problems with fogging glasses and we expected, other unspecified annoyances. He promptly sat down, removed his pack and declared a trekker's strike, in agitated despair. Larry and I attempted to discern the cause of his anguish, with no apparent source of annoyance other than his vapor affected specs. Why removing them had not occurred to him before our suggestion, no one knows. However, upon removal of his offending lenses, all was well with the world and the assent was on.

I know you have heard this from me before but, damn, that climb was hell! The weather deteriorated into gale strength winds, driving rain into our faces with violent force. Justin, now seemingly contented to gallop along his merry way, scampered out of sight up the mountain. I fell behind Larry and continued to labor at a snail's pace. Soon I was on my own, 10 paces then stop to rest. My mind and body were just not ready for the task at hand. At one moment the rain and wind were pounding me relentlessly and my legs, reminiscent of the "Royal Navy step over", refused to go any further. I leaned against the mountainside, surrendering to all of the forces involved, content to remain a fixture for as long as need be.

I regrouped and renewed my feeble upward assault (I really should try to get in shape before our next trip). The weather slacked, and as I rounded a left bend in the trail. Thank God...Larry and Justin sat against the trail junction sign just ahead. Only 1.1 miles to the Clingmans Dome parking lot, and our waiting van.

It was shortly after this point that I finally, after all of our trips, earned my trail nickname. The trail actually becomes several feet deep and just a couple feet wide worn into solid rock. It is not easy to walk in the rut itself, so I walked just to the side of the trail. Larry and Justin led by about 20 yards. Suddenly I lost my balance, fell backward, and wedged my pack right smack dab in the rock rut. I realized quite astutely that without assistance, extraction from my precarious position would be difficult at best. Calling for assistance, I began to move my arms and legs, trying my best to pull free. Yep, picture a turtle upside down, trying desperately to right himself. Luckily Justin and Larry saw my dilemma from their forward position and returned to laughingly lend a hand. Thus I became "Flailing Turtle".

Larry and I sat, telling these tales of adventure to Mom and Dad one night, as we often did, Dad remarked that we sure seemed to have a great time out on the trail.

"You want to give it a try with us?" I ask instinctively.

"I don't think your dad needs to be out hiking through those mountains at 68 years old." Mom quickly threw in her two cents.

She was usually quick to slow our adventure train, especially where Dad was involved. She did have some reason for her concerns, as they pertain to his health. Allow me to stray in that direction for a brief moment.

Let's go back 20 years earlier. Dad was walking across the street from the county courthouse during the course of his workday, when he felt something was just not quite right. His left arm felt a slight twinge of discomfort. Once back at his office, he was driven to our local hospital due to the concerned urgings of a good friend and co-worker. Evidence of a heart attack was detected, and he was sent to the Cleveland Clinic for proper evaluation and treatment.

Back then local hospitals weren't equipped to handle such problems. Once admitted, tests were done. The prognosis was not good. Mom didn't drive much in those days, and we sons took turns driving her the 60 miles to the clinic. I remember Mom crying as she left his room and told us to go in. Dad wanted to talk to us. The three of us walked into that room knowing darn well that things were probably not good. That may be the only time I saw tears in his eyes. It's the only time I can remember. Four arteries were not only severely blocked but pretty much deteriorated to the point that there may be no fixing the problem. He was not ready to go and we all left that night with heavy hearts and feelings of dread.

What the heck! All my life this man was up at 4:30 in the morning. He would do calisthenics, shower, shave (while singing "Streets of Laredo" or other western ballads), read the Bible, and eat his bowl of cereal. Then he would go to work. That was every day but Sunday for as long as I could remember. How could he have heart problems at such a young age?

The next day Dr. Toby Cosgrove entered my Dad's hospital room. He told Dad he could perform the procedures needed to keep his heart going, hopefully for the next 15 years. The doctor was good to his word. It was a long recovery, but 20 years later...well, thank the good Lord and Dr. Cosgrove. Back to our story.

"I don't think that's a very smart idea, " Mom said.

"Oh, stop being so dramatic" Dad threw out in promising reply.

"Well, he has walked 2 miles every morning for the last 20 years and he has checked out just fine with his doctors. Besides we can put together a reasonably easy route" Larry wisely added. "We can stay along Fontana Lake and maybe fish the lake and tributary streams."

Mom just shook her head, in partial surrender to our customary stupidity. We actually won that exchange!

All 5 of us piled out of the van in the parking lot at the end of Lakeview Dive. With the needed fishing licenses procured in Bryson City, we were more than ready to get started. Grandsons Matt and Justin, and their grandpa Richard joined Larry and myself on this 3 generations hike. Dad was excited to be a part of it all. We were thrilled to share a piece of our world with him. The day was warm and beautiful as we stepped to it.

So Lakeview Drive is often referred to as the Road to Nowhere. Started in the 1960's, it was to connect the eastern side of the mountains from Bryson City to Fontana Village. The road is now closed at the parking area where we now parked. However, the pavement continues for several hundred yards to the other side of the tunnel which we were about to enter. There are few things more inviting to young boys, and even some of us older ones, then just about anything abandoned. I can't explain it, just the way it is.

Now this tunnel is long, dark, and damp. At 375 yards in length, the light at the end of the tunnel is not just a figure of speech, but a very small and dim point of reference, marking the end of this unfulfilled relic of forsaken construction. Once inside, there is of course, some of the ever present graffiti. But the tunnel structure, the impressive length, and it's slow but continuous state of deterioration are the eye-catching attributes. We all advanced with flashlights

Illuminating the dark and mysterious secrets within. A few bats, spiders, seeping water, and a dead possum added to the ambiance.

We emerged from the domed inky darkness into the sunlit, leaf strewn forest on the far side of the subterranean passage, embraced by the unconfined natural beauty of the open trail. Ground rules were reasserted as to the "Rabbits" absolute adherence to mandatory (stop and wait) halts at all trail intersections, marked or not. All checks completed, it was time to let the fun begin.

The boys readily left us behind as they scampered down the trail. Dad took to 'backpack life" as if it was second nature. He was using the old Camp Trails frame pack I purchased 7 years previously for our first Clingmans Dome trip, and it suited him well. He had procured a pair of lightweight hiking shoes and we outfitted his other gear needs. At 68, he appeared to be at ease and quite comfortable as he strode forward between Larry and myself. We were impressed to say the least.

Just about 1.25 miles in, Larry stopped for a breather as we topped a 100' rise. You probably guessed by now, while I was a bit tired and needed to down considerable water, and Larry's knees were feeling the burn just a little, the "old guy" wondered why we stopped at that point. I told him to be sure to take a drink to hydrate. He said he was good and smiled as he mentioned we might want to take it a bit slower in concern for our winded appearance. I thought he was too old to be a smart ass. I was wrong.

This trip would be the first time I realized where Larry got his diminished need for water. Dad obviously passed this trait on to him. Heck, both can exert themselves for hours without taking more than a sip. I go through a good quart and a half while they consume a pint. On a warm day such as this, I find it baffling. Both are like camels.

There were several trail junctions and the Rabbits would be sitting against the marker post, dutifully awaiting our arrival. At each stop, we pulled out the map and plotted the next section. Course set, they were immediately off breaking trail for our party and scouting on their own. They felt like Lewis and Clark leading the Corps of Discovery Expedition!

It was a beautiful 3 1/4- mile day when we reached our objective, beloved camp #74 (Lower Forney). Justin, Larry, and I had just been there a year prior, but it was new to Dad and Matt. Both were impressed as we threw our gear down fifteen feet from Forney Creek's thundering waters. A fire pit and large river boulders lent a certain rustic charm to our home for the next 2 nights .The usual woodsy charms of the October Smokies permeated camp - the earthy smells and pleasant crunch of ankle deep fallen leaves, the fresh damp aroma and tumbling roar of the clear mountain creek, the enticing perfume and hushed whisperings of tall pines swaying in the gentle late afternoon breeze. Yes...the stuff dreams are made of.

We easily prepared our two- tent camp. Dad, Justin, and I slumbered in the trusty Eureka Timberline. Matt and Larry tried out a new Walrus two-man tent, a welcomed improvement over their "tiny tent episode". The kitchen was set up beside a large, placid, pool, just perfect for gathering water. There were plenty of large rocks available for backrests. All the comforts we could ask of a backwoods fishing camp. Once again, all to ourselves.

It doesn't always happen that way. Just two years ago, Justin, Larry, and I took another fall run at #74. As we rested around our experimental hammock camp, late in the

morning, around 35 middle school students came
screaming into view on a science field trip! The teacher
apologized for their intrusion on our solitude. We told him
to carry on as there could be few better outings school kids
could wish for. You aren't always lucky enough to be
alone.

As the evening air cooled, we all enjoyed the warmth of
a good meal. Dad thought us to be top notch guides due to
our superior ability to provide such delicious fare. We all
devoured the beef stroganoff. Dad had a smile on his face
as he watched grandsons explore the lakeshore, as shadows
lengthened and the chill of sunset settled into our valley.
Steaming cups of coffee and coco by candle lantern light
accompanied conversation of the day's events. Soon
candles were snuffed and we all lost consciousness to the
rumble of Forney Creek serenade.

Larry and I had coffee by 6am, well before our 3 mates
showed their faces. The surprise being dad, Mr. 4am, not
showing until a half hour later. His Ridgerest/Slumberjack
bed must have suited him just fine. The youngest duo soon
followed. With nothing to do but fish, explore, and laze
around camp, we were in no particular hurry. Two nights in
the same trail camp was unusual for us. Leisurely mornings
were rare. A second cup of coffee countered the morning

cold. Once again, Matt protested the volume of my snoring which, according to him, even drowned out the deafening river. Larry collaborated, adding that the 20' between our tents was not near enough space. Justin chimed in, agreeing with their negative judgments while also throwing his grandfather under the bus. Welcome to camp, Dad.

Everything was cleaned and straightened, food re-hung, and fishing gear readied for our morning's watery assault. We all had ultra- light rods and reels, and an assortment of flies and small spinners. The trout had nowhere to hide!

Larry and Matt concentrated closer to camp and the lake's inlet. Justin and I left Dad just below Bear Creek while we tried Bear Creek, and a little higher up Forney. Four hours of fishing proved to be fruitless. Justin had tired of fishing, and went on a close by scouting mission. I refused to succumb to fishing failure. I continued floating flies downstream around every rock in sight as we made our way back to #74.

It was obvious we weren't having fish for lunch, as I rejoined the other empty hands back in camp. We all slumped against our backpack recliner rocks showing our obvious exhaustion from the morning's strenuous work. A pot of our favorite minestrone soup only added to forest lethargy. Dad settled in for an afternoon nap, Larry went to

work on a set of walnut knife handles he was making, and I
went down to the lake ready to prove myself a worthy
fisherman. The boys wanted to explore a game trail that ran
the eastern hillside along the lake. Within sight and
shouting distance, and away from the water, as set by the
ground rules. I strongly urged Justin, being older than his
cousin, to take the lead and keep all actions under control.

The day was now becoming cloudy and cool. After a
while Larry and Dad came down to the lake trying their
luck. The boys would periodically pop out of the trees
along the steep banks above the water's edge, give a quick
wave or yell, and duck back out of sight.

The three of us tossed spinners and various lures to no
avail. I could not understand why brochures about Fontana
Lake fail to mention the lack of fish within its
depths...serious omission. I expect it could be, as I may
have mentioned before, that I suck at fishing. I will not
speak for the others.

As the afternoon waned, we headed back to the homey
comforts of camp. I walked up stream, giving the flies just
one more chance to land a prize. Dad and Larry decided to
lounge in camp preparing for dinner.

As afternoon dwindled, cold settled in and I deemed my
angling foray a bust. Arriving in camp, I was just in time to

witness the inevitable. Larry loudly admonished our sons'
precarious streamside situation. His berating was just a hair
late, as Matt leaped from their steeply sloping bank onto a
"log island". Promptly his feet relinquished their hold on
that slippery wooden platform. Matt thrashed and splashed
in his quest for dry ground. Larry ran around camp and up
the hillside looking for the game trail leading to the scene
of the incident. Justin was yelling to Matt as he worked for
a useful means of extracation. I meanwhile yelled for Justin
to help Matt to safety without following in Matt's soggy
footsteps. Matt made safe ground with Justin's knee deep
assistance. Larry met them on the trail, as they made it half
way back to camp.

Larry was still sternly berating Matt for his foolish
antics as they appeared in camp. I instantly joined in the
fatherly reprimands, hounding Justin's lack of leadership
control. Although Justin rightly informed me that short of
roping and hogtying, Matt was going for the plunge. He
was right of course, and I came around to his point of view.
All the while Dad, aka Grandpa, sat back, strangely
enough, enjoying the ruckus. I guess he was entertained by
two of the knuckleheads he dealt with for years, handling
fatherly dilemmas of their own. Come to think of it, that is
what grand parenting should be.

Once dripping clothes hung on tree limbs, soaked boots dried by the fire, (that was necessary this night), the boys warmed, wrapped in sleeping bags. We downed warm hot chocolate. It only took a few minutes for this traumatic event to become a laughable source of evening entertainment. Sorry Matt, just a little humor at your expense! Good food, good company, good euchre, clear skies, the perfect night in good old Camp #74.

We said our farewells to Forney Creek and Fontana Lake the next morning. We had 4.4 miles ahead of us before spending a night at #67 (Goldmine Branch). No hurry as the miles were not too difficult. The first 1.5 miles would be a 500' rise, with fairly flat middle section, leading to an easy downhill finish. Area history was visible in the form of rock piles and old chimneys in a few spots along the way. Despite the name of the creek, we saw no evidence of early mining activities.

The trail dropped into a draw. We were welcomed by flat open terrain of our night's refuge. Justin and Matt found a great place capable of holding four sleeping bags, while affording an open view of the night sky. We really wanted to give Dad the opportunity to sleep under the stars, and it looked like tonight would serve us well.

Have you ever been at least just a little confused by actions contrary to your life long perceptions? As long as I can remember, Dad has hardly ever been in anything but suits and ties or at least, what I would call dress slacks and button down shirts. He was office bound 6 days a week and was on so many boards that many evenings he was working late. He was intensely driven by responsibility to community and family. I don't think it was easy for him to completely let things go and slow down. But right there, right then, hanging in the forest, dirty, unshaven, sleeping on the ground, just eating, sleeping and walking through the woods, well...it was like he was born for it. Now, don't get me wrong, he had his share of adventures as a lad growing up on a small farm in Holmes County Ohio as well as in his Air Force days. He was a mechanic on the post WWII Boeing B-50 Superfortress bomber. He tells some hair raising tales of flying home on leave a few times with a fellow airman in an open cockpit Ryan PT-22. The PT-22 was the first mono wing trainer the Air Force used. It was a bit underpowered and known to be somewhat temperamental to fly. On one occasion, they ran out of fuel and were lucky to find an open field which they used for a glide- in landing at a very opportune time. After obtaining adequate fuel, they took off barely clearing a barn in the line of take off only to miss a water tower by several feet! We do question, as does he, the decision to climb into this guy's plane on more than one occasion! Oh well, back to the woods.

That last night, the 5 of us, arms behind our heads, watched the twinkling heavens. Constellations and occasional shooting stars were dramatic entertainment. It was the kind of cold, still, clear night that seemed to brighten the same stars to an intensity greater than usual. The backwoods with its lack of light pollution was, of course, a crucial and welcomed factor. Extended night vision is also the reason Larry and I mostly prefer a fireless camp. There are few better ways to drift off to sleep.

With no need to conserve rations, breakfast was an extravaganza of eggs, bacon, and pancakes. With a short 2 mile hike back to the van, there was no need to hurry. Breakfast and packing were completed at a leisurely pace. Gear packed, strapped, mounted and belted, we were off, Rabbits leading the way.

We opted to remain under the open, sunny sky, forgoing a return venture through that interesting but forsaken tunnel. Stepping from the Tunnel Bypass trail back onto pavement, the foot travel was complete. Packs and boots were removed and stowed in the back of the van. We all sat taking in the sights and smells which we had enjoyed the last few days. We all re-energized, with cool water, beef sticks and granola.

As pointed out earlier, post hike protocol demanded an exit hotel and restaurant. Availability of steaks and beer could not be overlooked. Sharing all aspects of our usual customary activities with Dad was a priority. We hoped he would garner similar feelings of enjoyment we have felt each and every outing. This phase of the process had become an integral cool-down time of reflection, and physical relaxation. Am I right...eat, drink and be merry! Hey, it's in the Bible.

Yep, three generations overeating and laughing while recalling tales of the trail. The kind of times thoroughly enjoyed and not to be forgotten. We all had a great time. Having Dad as one of the guys was a blessing.

We will never forget this special chance for trail camaraderie. Dad definitely proved to be up to the new challenge of backpacking. Justin and Matt continued to grow as woods dwellers. Fish continued to plot against our angling advances. Flowing waters certainly added to our outdoor adventure. The old lesson was again proven, young boys cannot be trusted around any such waters. Sharing an important part of your life with loved ones heightens and enriches the shared activity and appreciation for those companions. Dad definitely beat the odds in life and health.

Thanks for walking this road with us, Dad.

Chapter 10

Turkey, Downed Plane, and Bailing Out

I was not a happy camper, "What the hell."

"You didn't," Larry sounded as disappointed as I sounded ticked off.

"Yes...I just dropped the bolt down the oil galley!"

Larry had pulled the top end off of the motor on his 1987 Porsche 944, to get the valves worked. I was helping him reassemble it. Well, as you see, I was meaning to help. Picture if you can, the 2 of us looking down a dark small opening in the top of the motor. I, sick with the realization that my clumsy fingers may have caused more work than we ever wanted to tackle at the moment. Larry, silently wondering how to extract the bolt from its resting place and why the heck he had open the door when I showed up in the first place.

A telescoping magnet and Larry's steady hands retrieved the bolt and lifted the dread blanketing the atmosphere in that garage. Beers of triumph in hand, we once again relaxed in conversation.

"What would you say about getting Sarah down to the Smokies? I asked. "She finally has a break coming around Thanksgiving."

 Larry thought a second. "That would be cool. I can check with Matt. Maybe he and Justin can go."

Thus the planning gears started to mesh. Sarah's first mountain backpacking trip just might finally happen.

Sarah was born in July of 1996. Two weeks later she was in the backseat of our 1993 Ford Escort on the way to Arizona with Dee and myself, on one of my business trips. At two months she was rock hounding with Jaclyn and Justin in the North Carolina mountains. She has been camping and traveling ever since. Being as she was our daughter, her life did have a few preset priorities...beaches of North and South Carolina, rock hounding, camping, fishing, hiking, and hunting. When Sarah was two, Dee,

Justin, Jaclyn, and I took her on a trip West. We camped in Badlands National Park in South Dakota, Vernal, Utah (Dinosaur National Monument), the Pioneer Mountains in Montana...anyway, a lot of places visited and activities experienced. I'm trying to say, she had many adventures in her own right as a young girl.

Then Jr. High and sports seemed to consume practically all of her time. We still hit the beach at Ocean Isle, North Carolina each spring with 15 or so family members. Those trips have given us great times to remember. However, basketball, track, softball, jr. rifle club, and tennis took over. We do like sports, and Sarah loved them all. Between regular seasons and off- season camps, she stayed pretty well booked. Dee and I also had jobs with only so much holiday and vacation time available. We were lucky to have the luxury of having those days to play with, and we took full advantage.

I would sneak off on my mentally medicinal pack trips when I could. Dee would hold down the fort and the two of them would have a girl fest, free to enjoy life without the "grumpy old man" around.

I wanted to give Sarah a taste of life on the trail, preferably in higher elevations. Now was the time. She was 11, and it looked like basketball would break just long enough for a few days on the trail. Only one problem, it would have to be over Thanksgiving. Our usual tradition would involve a turkey on the grill and having family over. It is one of my favorite holidays.

Larry, Justin, Sarah, and I all figured it was now or never. Unfortunately, Matt couldn't make the run with us, due to previous commitments. We mapped out a quick, but ambitious (for us old guys), three day 15- mile trip out of Cosby campground, up Low Gap Trail to the Appalachian Trail and Cosby Knob Shelter. Then we would hike west on the AT, and down Camel Gap Trail into North Carolina, east on Gunter Fork Trail to #37 (Lower Walnut Bottom), then north on Low Gap trail back up to the AT, over the gap and back down to Cosby.

We chose this particular route for a couple of reasons. Larry, Matt, Justin, and I had done the first half of this route many years before. It gave us ups, downs, high ridges, and valleys with nice streams. Also, if we detoured just a few hundred yards further up the AT before heading down Camel Gap Trail, there is wreckage of an Air Force jet scattered up the mountainside, visible on both sides of the trail. Dee, Sarah, and I are all aviation admirers, and I was sure Sarah would find the site very interesting.

Sarah was seriously geared-up with a new internal frame pack and sleeping bag. She was feeling it. It's all she talked about for a week leading up to departure. Justin was also raring to get back to the mountains and life on the trail. We had not been on a trip together for several years. Thanksgiving at altitude sure sounded like a fun diversion. It was a shame Matt could not make the trek.

Despite recent knee and back problems, Larry was excited for another run at the November mountains. Scans revealed a floating piece of bone in his back, that could touch off pain through his hip and at times down through his knee. Our hope was that such occurrences remained at bay. Fingers crossed.

Thanksgiving Day 2007 dawned around us as we readied for our festive holiday excursion on foot. Larry expressed concern as packs were strapped on. The 500 mile 8 hour ride down did his back no favor. Sciatica had been giving him severe pain in his back, hips and down his leg on occasions leading up to the trip. The first part of our day started in the campground parking area. From there Low Gap Trail climbed around 1900' in just under 3 miles. Larry and I exchanged questioning glances as we looked up the steep grade of our trail's visible start. Oh well, here we go.

A mile and a half and 950' into our initial climb, I caught up with Larry, resting beside the trail.

"I'm not sure I can make these next 3 days," he voiced doubt, "I may have to go back down and either stay in the van or find a hotel until you guys finish."

I assured him all in or none in. If he needed to head back we would all bail and change plans, whatever the situation necessitated. At this point I was pleasantly surprised just how good I felt on this climb. After a break, Larry decided to forge on, hoping things would feel better as time went on.

We all regrouped at the snowy trail intersection in Low Gap. Sarah and Justin were waiting for us, de-geared, with jerky in hand. Larry and I both stumbled to a halt and joined the other two, reclined and relaxed. Honestly, I believe everyone was glad that climb was behind us. We had a little less than a mile with 500' of elevation gain to Cosby Knob Shelter, our Thanksgiving Day lodge.

Dreary and cold became the theme of the day. Snow and ice covered much of the afternoon's trail. However, spirits remained high at the thought of soon being at the shelter. Sarah was particularly excited for her first self-propelled high-country camp. Entering the shelter clearing, we were surprised to find a newly constructed, covered eating area in front of the sleeping shelter itself. A cooking table lined the left outside wall. Sleeping would be on a solid wood bunk area, large enough for 12. We hoped, as usual to have solitude during our stay. It would be a cozy, handy home for the night.

We immediately laid out our bedding to loft, and gear was readied for Thanksgiving dinner preparations. For those not familiar with camping gear, lightweight sleeping bags are filled with airy synthetic fibers or natural feather down. When packed for the trail, the bag is tightly compressed into a stuff sack, thus saving space. In camp, the bag should be removed from the stuff sack and shaken out to "loft" or separate the fill. This creates air pockets, intended to trap and hold body heat. Yes, loft is important.

A stiff cold breeze whipped through camp as we went about our chores. Sarah and Justin replenished our water supply and filled cooking pots from the nearby spring, while Larry and I set up the stoves for cooking. We all gathered about the kitchen, eager for the feast. Sliced turkey with gravy, mashed potatoes, green beans and stuffing were all on the menu. Oh yeah, blueberry cobbler to top it all off. Thank the hiking gods for dehydrated food! The Pilgrims would have been proud. We all gave thanks for...making it here first of all...being here...our companionship, and good food(considering). We were also thankful that without the usual football game to watch, we enjoyed the beautiful view of the valley steeply dropping before us, lending distant forest and mountain views through leafless limbs. This was a different and very special Thanksgiving for all of us.

Temps continued to drop as darkness engulfed our humble abode. Of course being late November, and considering we were on the east side and below the ridge, daylight disappeared quickly and early. That fact dictated warm sleeping bags, headlamps, candle lanterns, and hot drinks, imperative for the obligatory euchre game. Sarah got her euchre baptism by fire that night. She was a quick study and soon she and I were giving Larry and Justin all they could handle. Being the only ones in camp, boisterous laughter and card slamming plays echoed throughout the clearing. Damn, that was a fun evening! Knowing it would be a long cold night, play was extended for as long as our exhaustion would allow. Several games later, candles were extinguished, headlamps switched off and everyone zipped in for the duration. That was one cold night.

Shivering, I lit the stove before dawn, eager for my first warming cup of coffee. A dip into the 20s sent our cozy camp into the arctic zone. Soon everyone was up and moving, bleary eyed but ready to partake of a steaming drink and hot breakfast. A few stretches and jumping jacks, assisted in adding warmth and lifting spirits. The first hint of daylight only seemed to drop temps and accentuate the morning chill. We hoped and dreamed of bright, warming sunshine peeking into our camp from the southeastern sky. These hopes were soon dashed as dawn exposed a sunless, cloudy sky. Oh well, the morning's mountain walk would soon boost internal warmth to reasonable levels.

In just under a mile, we would crest over 5000' before descending a few hundred feet over the next mile, where we would intersect Camel Gap Trail. Departure came with some sadness, as we had experienced a fine holiday gathering within this lofty getaway. But, it was time to push on to our next objective. The trail was snow covered, and a cold damp fog engulfed the flora shrouded pathway. The insidious fog drove the cold clear to the bone. However, I hiked in a t- shirt and an insulated flannel shirt. Sweat soaked both of my shirts early into the trek. Larry experienced similar symptoms. Justin as always, dressed as an Eskimo, quite different from myself. Sarah was also pretty well bundled.

At one point we dropped to rest on a steep snow covered incline. As we rested, packs unhitched, Justin spotted tracks cutting our trail several feet in front of us. Justin investigated and found a nice sized bear had crossed our path from north to south. They appeared to be fresh, thus we heightened our awareness, hoping for a glimpse of the bruin.

"I thought you said we didn't have far to go this morning?" Sarah questioned.

"We just got started. We just got going" I answered with annoyance. "Should be just ahead a half mile or so."

On up the trail, which I will admit seemed to continue longer than I remembered, Sarah reminded me of my previous statement concerning the short distance to the junction.

"I thought you said it was close" she chided.

Looking up the steep trail, I added. "See that open sky at the high point ahead? We will bend left and drop down to the trail sign."

"How many times have I heard that already," she caustically replied.

Slogging ahead, I relished the thought of bending left and jabbing her with a well deserved I told you so. Rounding the turn ahead of me, Sarah stopped and waited. I reached her only to see the angry look on her face and the same shrouded walkway winding ever upward. Damn, memory had failed me again. This trail did seem to go on forever...must be the cold. I pleaded my case, being map, direction, and memory challenged. All to no avail. Although not put in the exact words, I remember being referred to as a disappointment of sorts...Daughters!

I was relieved as we finally made it to Camel Gap. Now maybe I would regain some trekking respect. No, I haven't lived that two mile ordeal down to this day! Oh well, broad shoulders.

The gap did offer some good views to the north. Of course, we enjoyed the vista and took some pictures. Larry was having a rough time with his back. He was hinting strongly of doubts concerning his completion of the rest of our intended route.

Larry stayed at the junction to give his back a needed break while Sarah, Justin, and I made our way up to the crash site. A few hundred yards brought us to solemn ground. We gave a moment of reflection for the 2 men who lost their lives in this violent event.

I have read the account of this incident in the book: *Mayday! Mayday! Aircraft Crashes in the Great Smoky Mountains National Park 1920-2000* by Jeff Wadley and Dwight McCarter. These two along with so many others, have put their lives on the line at a moment's notice, in order to search for and rescue survivors or recover the deceased occupants of downed aircraft within the Park, often under severely adverse weather conditions. I can only imagine the physical, mental, and emotional toll these selfless searchers have experienced. I am in awe of their efforts. The book is very interesting, compelling, and I highly recommend it. According to their account, this Air Force F4 Phantom II (RF-4C reconnaissance jet) piloted by Capt. David F. Greggs and navigated by Capt. Scott A. Miller was flying a night training mission on January 4, 1984. For reasons unknown, the plane slammed into Inadu

Knob at 5850', killing both crewmen. Crash debris is scattered over almost 20 acres.

It is not often that one can view an aircraft crash site in a backcountry setting (or any other actually). The three of us spent some time combing a draw on both sides of the trail. Finding a section of cockpit with seat still somewhat intact was quite sobering. We found partial control sections with actuators still attached. Fuselage sections, hydraulic equipment, and pieces we couldn't identify were present. Viewing this wreckage was exciting, thought provoking, and somewhat depressing, all at the same time. Having been to the site twice, I still am intrigued with it. Sarah has recently told me that she wants to visit the site in the future for further investigation. I hope we can make the trip together.

Back at the trail junction we sat for a break. Larry was checking the map.

"Well guys, my back can no way make the rest of the trip. I'm afraid after finishing today I couldn't make the climb back up to Low Gap tomorrow. You go ahead and I'll head back to the van and crash there until you come out tomorrow."

None of us liked the idea of Larry hiking out alone. What if his back gave out before he made it? He would surely need my expert medical assistance. Besides, we were all thinking that helping a comrade in trouble was better than climbing back to Low Gap for ourselves. Hell, the thought of a quick exit, certainty of a nice bed, a big steak and a very large beer wasn't all that bad either. Yes, it became clear that we must think of Larry, his health, comfort, and well- being. There, decision made. Take the high road! Time to bail out!

Having an alternate objective (read as large steak) in sight, we all started to don our packs. Suddenly out of nowhere, two large, black hounds came bounding into our midst. Tails wagging, they greeted each of us as if we were long lost friends. Each wore an orange collar equipped with a tracker and tags. Figuring their people were close by, we told them to stay then we hit the AT, figuring to drop down Snake Den Ridge Trail. Yes, the same trail I went hypo-stupid and Larry did his best puppet impression in 1994. We very much hoped that particular crossing would be in a much safer condition today. We trudged on and the hounds followed. Soon the Alpha dog was leading our way while the other stayed by our side.

At the intersection with Snake Den Ridge, we checked for phone service. None to be had. Both dogs had the owner's name and phone number. We now figured they were separated, and contact was the best plan of action, but it would have to wait.

Just 4.6 miles of winding downhill trail to go. Larry was really feeling the hurt now, but continued to gut it out. Not much choice of course. I showed Sarah and Justin our infamous blizzard camp. The six of us, dogs included, continued on until we came to the water crossing. Not a water crossing..."the water crossing of death"! We took a break as Larry and I painted a picture of the death defying feats of our past icy descent.

At this time, I must point out that we had brought Justin and Matt up this same trail several years ago. Approaching this same crossing from the other direction, we had stopped to remove socks and shoes in order to wade the much shallower obstacle. I had admonished Justin to wait for our assistance. We heard a gasping shriek and looked up just in time to see Justin half way across, bent over, yet still on his feet, head submerged, held under by the weight of his pack, which had rocked forward on his shoulders. What a sight, both hands in the water, holding him from somersaulting into the drink, but without enough arm-length to propel him back, erect. I quickly came to his assistance, righting his posture as I (thoughtfully) hurled an I told you so. He, of course, let me know my concerns and assistance were not needed as he was about to extract himself from the predicament. Anyway, we all had a good laugh at his expense. He even got a smile out of it.

After telling Sarah that same story, we all rolled up our pants, removed socks and shoes, and waded across the knee- deep, freezing water. On the other side, legs and feet were hurriedly dried, and socks and shoes refitted. A cold but uneventful crossing. That hurdle cleared, on we went, wet shaking dogs and all.

As usual, this downhill, root- bound trail took its toll on us all. Larry for sure. It seemed to wind on forever. Then again, you have heard that story too many times before. None of us appeared to be at our physical peak this trip. We finally stumbled out of the forest and into the Cosby parking area. All were glad to be off our feet. Larry was especially ready for a cushy van seat. His back was screaming for a reprieve. With phone service restored, we contacted the dogs' owner who just happened to live on the other side of the mountain. They would be quickly on their way to pick them up. We hoped the hounds would still be there.

As per our revised plan, a decent hotel with a handy close by dining establishment was procured for the night. We clinked glasses to a fun although somewhat painful trip. Fried onions, salads, steaks and laughs revived us as we reminisced on the events of the last few days. Heck, this had become an important aspect of our outings. Humor at all of our expenses flowed freely and everyone was glad to surrender their humility. We were, after all, companions of the trail.

Thanksgiving observed while backpacking high in the Smokies was a wonderful experience. To have such an event with two of my kids and one of my brothers was pretty special. Larry and I are lucky to have spouses that understand our desire to be in the mountains and on the trail. It is a gift many never get to experience. Obviously the true reward is not really in the finish of any one particular route. It's not like we through hiked the AT or anything like that. Just being out in nature with like minded companions to share the adventure is the true reward.

Chapter 11

Insights

I would like to tell you why I love the Smoky Mountains so much, but I'm not sure I can put it into words. They have impacted my life and impressed me more than anywhere else I have been. For instance, the Rocky Mountain Range is absolutely beautiful and has peaks over 14,000'. Don't get me wrong here, I do love the Rockies. I have spent a fair amount of time in them. But the Smokies, in my mind, are something very special.

The biodiversity within the park is now 19,000 species of plants, animals, and fungi. And scientists believe there are 80,000 to 100,000 additional, still waiting for discovery (NPS.GOV). It is one of the most diverse, temperate zones in the world. We have seen herds of over 100 deer in Cades Cove. There are also turkeys, elk, coyotes, wild boars and black bears, just to name some of the animals. Larry and I recall there were around 400 to 450 black bears within the park when we first started hiking there, now, they number 1500. That's 2 bears per square mile. We have seen a few but not as many as you might think.

At times I get an eerie feeling of the history I am treading on as walk through one of the oldest mountain ranges on earth. The Cherokee Nation did roam the Smokies and the home of The Eastern Band of the Cherokees still reside at the foot of the North Carolina side of the mountains. The town of Cherokee is an interesting, educational and entertaining place to visit.

As I was writing this I realized I never put a pack on my back until I was 31 years old. I never really thought about it in those terms. I had also never been to The Great Smoky Mountain National park until then. I may have been a late bloomer as far as backpacking and knowledge of the Smokies but I did my best to make up for lost time.

Not everyone is able to, or even wishes to, enjoy the same kinds of experiences that I have. Then again, I'm not saying backpacking or visiting The Great Smoky National Park are the only means to a fulfilling life. Quite the contrary. While both have been, and hopefully will continue to be, an extremely spiritual part of mine, everyone can find their own "mountain" retreat, in their own way. Life is only what you make it. Grab hold of it...Experience it...Celebrate it. Get out there, wherever there is for you, and make life worth living. It is your choice. It truly is all about the journey. And, if your mountain just happens to be in the Smokies...I hope this unexceptional hiker meets you, on the trail.

Special Thanks to my co-author and constant
companion while writing this book.

Sven Jäger Herald

www.ingramcontent.com/pod-product-compliance
Lightning Source LLC
Chambersburg PA
CBHW061753250726
48657CB00001B/97